Profile
of
Robert Frost

Compiled by

Lewis P. Simpson
Louisiana State University

Charles E. Merrill Publishing Company
A Bell & Howell Company
Columbus, Ohio

CHARLES E. MERRILL PROFILES

Under the General Editorship of
Matthew J. Bruccoli and Joseph Katz

ACKNOWLEDGEMENTS

From "Little Gidding" in Four Quartets. Copyright 1943, by T. S. Eliot. Reprinted by permission of Harcourt Brace Jovanovich, Inc.

From "The Figure A Poem Makes" from *Selected Prose of Robert Frost,* edited by Hyde Cox and Edward Connery Lathem. Copyright 1939, © 1967 by Holt, Rinehart, and Winston, Inc. Reprinted by permission of Holt, Rinehart and Winston, Inc. and Jonathan Cape, Ltd.

From *The Poetry of Robert Frost,* edited by Edward Connery Lathem. Copyright 1916, 1923, 1928, 1930, 1934, 1939, 1947, © 1969 by Holt, Rinehart and Winston, Inc. Copyright 1936, 1942, 1945, 1951, © 1956, 1958, 1962 by Robert Frost. Copyright 1964, 1967, 1970 by Lesley Frost Ballantine. Reprinted by permission of Holt, Rinehart and Winston, Inc. and Jonathan Cape, Ltd.

From *The Selected Letters of Robert Frost,* edited by Lawrence Thompson. Copyright 1964 by Holt, Rinehart and Winston, Inc. Reprinted by permission of Holt, Rinehart and Winston, Inc. and the estate of Robert Frost.

From "Tortoise Shout" and "Snake" from *The Complete Poems of D. H. Lawrence,* Volume I, edited by Vivian de Sola Pinto and E. Warren Roberts. Copyright 1923, renewed 1951 by Frieda Lawrence. Reprinted by permission of The Viking Press, Inc.

ISBN: 0-675-09234-5

Library of Congress Catalog Number: 78-143449

1 2 3 4 5 6 7 8 9—79 78 77 76 75 74 73 72 71

Printed in the United States of America

Introduction

This group of essays by American critics and scholars reflect contemporary thinking, and not less feeling, about Robert Frost and his poems. Selected, with one exception from leading American literary and scholarly magazines, each essay is complete in itself, none being a fragment divorced from a larger context. They are arranged in three sections. Those in the first emphasize images Frost made, and yet makes, in his role as a poet; those in the second deal with thematic and structural elements in Frost's poems. The last section offers one essay: a graphic summation by Alfred Kazin of the meaning of the poet and his work. The three parts of the reader are closely related. Indeed, the very division is meant strongly to suggest that a clear-cut distinction between Frost and his poems cannot be insisted upon. Understood in a relative way, it enables us to approach the study of a poet whose vocation to poetry was intensely self-conscious, and yet not lyrical but dramatic. In his own best known essay on poetry, Frost speaks of "The figure a poem makes." The figure his poems make, Frost's career implies, are the figures the poet makes; or, put the other way around, the figures the poet makes are the figures his poems make. Reading the essays presented here we can begin to trace the complex Frostian figuration in the realm of poetry.

Undertaking such a delineation, we become aware of a problematical but fundamental relationship between Frost as a figure of the American poet and Frost as a figure of the modern poet. A few suggestions about this relationship with reference to the essays in this reader may be helpful.

A primary problem in the evaluation of Frost is his large public image as the American poet incarnate. The greatest exception to the private role of the poet in American society, Frost's long-time national career was only given climactic confirmation in 1960 when he took part in the inauguration of a President. For forty years, Pulitzers and honorary degrees had fallen on him like the rain; he had been revered and pampered both on the American campus and off in a manner unlikely ever to be repeated.

Why Frost became a still treasured image of the poet as a national figure is no problem to the American public, which finds sufficient analyses of its motives in Gallup polls. But it has been and continues to be a problem to students of American poetry, who take themselves and poetry seriously, often very seriously. When Frost is taken seriously, he seems to involve a paradox. The age of public poets is well past. How can a poet of modern times be at once popular and important? The tendency of the student is to answer the question in a negative way. Any poet who is popular must be a fraud, or else his audience must favor him for the wrong reason; they take him, that is, for some image of common, and thus superficial, value. Lloyd N. Dendinger seeks to arrive at a positive, and comprehensive explanation of Frost's popular stature. For one thing, he points out, Frost was a perennial platform performer. He was a good actor; he entertained people. More essentially, his presence on the platform was that of the New England sage. A good deal must be made of the figure of the wise American Frost thus presented. In this image, which has carried over well past his death, he played an authoritative role long sanctioned by American culture. In spite of the conflicting claims of cultural superiority by the various regions of the United States, even in spite of the Civil War, New England continued on into the twentieth century to be considered synonomous with American literature. The South was as intimately associated with the genesis of the American Revolution and the founding of the Republic as New England, but New England had the poets, storytellers, and historians to make a national literature. For generations the most literate region of the country, its literary center and schoolroom, New England produced nearly all the classic American writers: Longfellow, Holmes, Lowell, Whittier, Emerson, Thoreau, Hawthorne. Owing to its literary achievement, it is not too much to say that New England came to represent the wisdom and moral virtue of being American. This virtue, peculiarly connected with the rural or pastoral life of New England, was proclaimed in a simple way by poems once found in every school book in America: Whittier's "Snow Bound," the idylls of Lowell and Holmes, Longfellow's "My Lost Youth" (the refrain of which suggested to Frost the title of his first book, *A Boy's Will*). In more complex ways, the New England description of American virtue was declared in Emerson's essays and in Thoreau's *Walden* (one of Frost's favorite books). New England rural life, in other words, cogently symbolized the integrity of the national life—which was, as established in Crèvecoeur's *Letters from an American Farmer* and Jefferson's *Notes on Virginia*—generally considered to be most truly represented by American ways of life in villages and on small farms and by the figures of the American villager and the farmer. Always existing in an implied contrast with types of debased life in Europe, the feudal peasant or the venal city dweller, they were the chief figures in an ideal American economy of virtue.

But the pastoral life in America, as Dendinger observes, had a broader dimension than its relation to farm and village. It had a primary relation to the great wilderness which was once America. The American was more aware of the relationship of the pastoral existence to the wilderness than he was of the relation of the pastoral way to the city, for he quite literally made his gardens in successive areas of virgin forests and wide prairies. The primary drive of the American, or so he imagined with Thomas Jefferson, was to transform a wilderness into a garden inhabited by self-sufficient yeomen. But in coming into the wild, the American developed a fascination with it, and the tension between the pastoral subjection of the wilderness and an affinity for the raw wildness of a primitive world created the conflict we see in Leatherstocking; or, for that matter, in Thoreau. The "traveller through the natural world" heard a call for a more radical freedom from civilization than that of the pastoral voice—this voice actually a civilizing one, urging that the woods be made into farm and village. He heard a summons from the virgin woods to enter into the mystery of a complete freedom from the power of the historical past and the tyranny of the present. To the extent that Americans, yesterday and today, have listened to the call of the wild, they have heard intimations of an integrity of existence closer to the profound instinctual roots of being than the pastoral life can offer. Such a profoundity of being is to be discovered in the woods dark and deep. So our fascinated response to Frost's most famous poem, "Stopping by Woods on a Snowy Evening." This is about the psychic situation of a traveller who stops on a darkening winter afternoon to watch a woods filling with snow. Tantalized by the promise of an escape into a condition beyond the reach of all established order, and yet always yielding to the necessity of order, the American identifies with the traveller in the natural world as he appears in the poem. This figure Dendinger sees as the central poetic image in Frost, an image of universal appeal to Americans.

In a discerning study of the figure of Frost—written when Frost was a living presence in America, appearing constantly before the sizeable and heterogeneous audiences he always drew—James M. Cox in "Robert Frost and the Edge of the Clearing" sees a more subjective shaping of the pastoral figure of Frost than Dendinger does. In the chaos of modern consciousness, Frost's role is analogous to that of the farmer who expands his realm into the adjacent woods; on the one side is wilderness, on the other an already domesticated area. Maintaining in his consciousness "the marginal world between the wild and the tame," Frost fulfills a psychic need of Americans. He plays a part in the agrarian myth of the nation.

But does Frost's portrayal of the lonely, independent "farmer poet" adequately fulfill the sensibility of "alienation" so central in the conception of the modern poet? Did Frost have an intense enough vision of his vocation under the conditions of modernity?

A long-standing quarrel about Frost's relevance to modern poetry exists. Lionel Trilling was aware of the quarrel when, in a famous address at the dinner given for Frost by his publisher on the occasion of his eighty-fifth birthday, he declared the poet to be imbued with the sensibility of the modern literary vocation. In spite of his reputation as a spokesman of official American culture, Trilling declared, Frost has perceived a terrifying vision both of America and the universe. Trilling's comments, which are considered by Dendinger and other essayists in this collection, brought down a barrage of condemnation by J. Donald Adams and like-minded critics devoted to extolling Frost as a spokesman of American values. But when he depicted Frost as a terrifying poet, Trilling probably did not have the J. Donald Adams end of the Frost critical spectrum so much in mind as he did that part occupied by more sophisticated critics of Frost like Yvor Winters and Malcolm Cowley. Standing on the assumptions of his oftentimes narrow critical puritanism, Winters accused Frost of being a "spiritual drifter"; in the spirit of the literary critic with a social conscience Cowley accused Frost of being an antiquarian. Taken either way Frost does not measure up to the demands modernity makes upon the poet. In an informed and trenchant criticism of Frost (written subsequent to the storm aroused by Trilling's depiction of Frost) Isadore Traschen sets forth a view of the poet's failings as a modern that is more comprehensive than either that of Winters or Cowley, and one that affords a thoughtful qualification of Trilling's attitude. Frost avoided a tragically heroic confrontation with his age. He talked about the desirability of the poet's searching for unity in the modern mind and spirit—affirming that the poet is "to say matter in terms of spirit, or spirit in terms of matter"—but he did not realize a controlling vision comparable to Eliot's vision of the waste land. He did not, like Eliot, go through the dark night of the soul necessary to a saving vision. Frost is a figure of the modern poet *manqué*.

The essays in the second section of the reader, however, present evidence that if Frost failed in projecting a unified vision of the modern world, he had strong intimations of the modern crisis of mind and spirit. Alvan S. Ryan's study of Frost's theory and practice of poetry in comparison to Emerson's points out how the poetry of Frost rests in a vision of nature, society, and evil closer to that of a modern writer like Robert Penn Warren than to that of his

New England predecessor. Warren's own essay argues that the basic theme of Frost's poetry lies in the dialectical interpenetration of the worlds of fact and dream, out of which the poet's insistent theme of self-definition emerges. Essentially rejecting this argument, Nina Baym contends that Frost's themes center on the realization that in nature "the grim laws of change and decay" rule. In a nonhuman universe, a poem is a gesture of the mind's resistance to the dynamism of decay, a figure of a meaningful human action. William H. Pritchard seeks to define the formative power in the figure Frost's poems make as a thorough-going modern pessimism about man's relationship with nature. Frost acknowledges a "diminished nature." Grasping the impossibility under modern conditions of the pathetic fallacy, he perceives the necessity of accepting a total difference between the mind and what lies outside the mind.

Frost's relation to the pastoral motive in the American imagination of man and nature may be more complex than we realize. The pastoral mode of the American consciousness, although its origins may not always be apparent, descends directly from the pastoral poems of Virgil, who first created in the Western mind a poetic landscape. In Virgil the primal world of Grecian pastoral becomes, as Bruno Snell shows in *The Discovery of the Mind,* a literary world of allegory and symbols; situated somewhere between myth and reality, it is a peculiar dominion of art. The poet, who appears in the guise of the shepherd, is the guardian of this world and the revealer of its mysteries. The history of Arcadia is lengthy and involved, and no portion of this is more intriguing, Leo Marx has demonstrated, than the special significance Arcadia took on in the American imagination. It became associated with the concept of America as a new Eden, a new creation, from which a novel myth of man and nature would emerge. Imagination operating upon the facts of America, the richness and diversity of the land, would bring man and nature into a new unity and redeem him from the long failure of his history. In spite of the massive historical evidence against it, this assumption of the pastoral destiny of America still persists in the American outlook. It accounts fundamentally, for example, for J. Donald Adams's attitude toward Frost at the time of the Trilling speech. Frost appeared to the New York *Times* critic to be almost a sacred figure in the mystery of the redemptive mission of America. Associating him with the European figure of the writer, Trilling had in effect committed an act of sacrilege. He had cast doubt upon the purity of Frost's priestly function in the preservation of American pastoral virtue.

The oversimplified image of Frost presented by J. Donald Adams is integrally related to a pessimistic image of our American poets discovered by more subtle American critics. They have found in American writers a decided gloominess about the redemptive connection between man and nature in America. They interpret American writers as understanding, indirectly if not directly, that the founding of the American Republic was coincident with the eruption of modern machines into history. The highly exploitative machine techniques of dealing with nature at once became standard procedure in the new nation. In this historical situation, instead of becoming a celebration of the pastoral achievement, American literature tended to become as much or more a lament for the destruction of the natural world and for the loss of the last chance for man to establish a redemptive harmony between himself and nature. This lament—the nostalgic cry of regret for "the lost woods"—runs through our writers from Cooper and Thoreau to Hemingway and Faulkner. It expresses what must be taken as a major attitude of American writers: a deep sense not only of discontent with industrial-technological civilization but of estrangement from its motives and purposes. At times the American writer's agonizing knowledge of the meaning of the loss of the woods becomes something like an eschatological vision. He is possessed of the fatal knowledge that the last chance for our salvation has been missed. The doom of the woods is our doom as well.

But—and this is rather startling—the figure of the American poet as a priest of nature under close scrutiny does not seem to be more than approximately close to the true figure of Robert Frost. One of the cardinal aspects of Frost is that he did not participate in either the myth of America as a new creation or in the eschatological myth of America as the lost and last chance. He does not set up in his poems the American writer's opposition between a pastoral and an industrial society. Unlike Faulkner, or the Southern Agrarians (who saw "Agrarian *versus* Industrial" as the chief issue of modern times), Frost is neither a keeper nor an elegist of the American garden—the visionary, transcendent homeland of the American spirit. Frost, it is more accurate to say, in the total implication of his poetry gives us a vision counter to one of man and nature unified. In his notable poem about the American destiny entitled "The Gift Outright," which he read from memory at the inauguration of President Kennedy, the point is made that the land belonged to the Americans before the Americans belonged to the land. If the sentiment seems to be based on the redemptive theme, it is because we deceive ourselves in wanting it to be rooted in an attitude we assume as an imperative. The poem develops the idea that the land possessed us not by the grace of the redemptive power of a new union with nature but by the strength of the human will exercised in the possession. The land now possesses us because we willed it to by "deeds of war." These deeds made the "deed of gift." The land was won by organized, institutional aggression of men against men in the name of a nationalizing people. We became the lands—made it "storied" and "artful"—by making it an integral part of our national history. To possess the land we did not become creatures of nature, who have no memory and no imagination. In "The Gift Outright" Frost pursues the same enveloping vision which informs his poems as a whole: a vision of the ironies of the unbridgeable and eternal separation of man and nature. Much of the underlying poignancy of Frost as an American poet lies in his implicit understanding of the illusion of America as the redemption of the world. Over against this apocalyptic vision he dramatizes a vision of existence in which man is man and the earth is the earth. Man wills the earth to be his home; he cannot do otherwise. Although the capacity of his will is great, it is finally no match for nature and we are always in danger of extinction.

To Frost, America was not a new chance or a last chance. He refused either version of America as the apocalypse of mankind. It is a version of the same chance man has always had. The definition of this chance in dramatic terms, the setting forth of its possibilities and its limitations, is what Frost, as he always put it, "says" in his poems. The figures he makes in saying this are the figures—the whole ironic configuration—the poet and his poems make in our imagination of America. Our imagination, Alfred Kazin makes dramatically clear in the last essay in this volume, of the hard won and precarious human order that is the Republic.

LEWIS P. SIMPSON

Baton Rouge, La.
November, 1970

Contents

Chronicle of Events

1874   (March 26) Robert Lee Frost born in San Francisco. Parents: William Prescott Frost, Jr. and Isabelle Moodie Frost

1885   Death of William Prescott Frost. Removal of Robert Frost's mother and children to New England, first to Lawrence, Massachusetts, and then to Salem, New Hampshire.

1888-92   Robert Frost attended Lawrence High School, graduated with highest honors. Briefly attended Dartmouth College.

1894-96   Frost pursued various occupations. Married to Elinor Miriam White in 1895. Began to publish poems in *The Independent*. First son, Elliott, born in 1896.

1897-1900   Attended Harvard as special student. First daughter, Lesley, born in 1899. Elliott Frost died in 1900.

1900-11   Frost moved with family to farm at Derry, New Hampshire. Second son, Carol, born in 1902; second daughter, Irma, born in 1903. Third daughter, Marjorie, born in 1905. Published various poems, including

	"The Trial by Existence." Taught at Pinkerton Academy, 1906-1911.
1912	Frost took up residence with his family in Beaconsfield, Buckinghamshire, England.
1913	*A Boy's Will* published in London.
1914	Frost moved with family to Gloucestershire. *North of Boston* published in London.
1915	Frost returned to United States. *North of Boston* and *A Boy's Will* published in New York. Bought farm in Franconia, New Hampshire.
1916	*Mountain Interval* published. Frost selected as Phi Beta Kappa Poet at Harvard. Elected to membership in the National Institute of Arts and Letters.
1917-20	Frost taught at Amherst College. Won *Poetry Magazine* prize for "Snow" in 1917. Moved to South Shaftesbury, Vermont, in 1920.
1921-22	Frost served at University of Michigan, Ann Arbor, as Poet-in-Residence and Fellow in Creative Arts.
1923	*Selected Poems* and *New Hampshire* published. Frost appointed Professor of English at Amherst College.
1924-25	Frost awarded Pulitzer Prize for *New Hampshire* in 1924. In 1925 held position as Fellow in Letters, University of Michigan.
1926	Took up post again as Professor of English at Amherst College, remained until 1938.
1928	*West-running Brook* published.
1930	*Collected Poems* published. Frost elected to American Academy of Arts and Letters.
1931	Frost awarded Pulitzer Prize for *Collected Poems*.
1932	Frost named Phi Beta Kappa Poet, Columbia University.
1934	Death of daughter, Marjorie.
1936	Frost named Charles Eliot Norton Professor of Poetry, Harvard University. *A Further Range* published; selected by Book-of-the-Month Club.
1937	Frost elected to American Philosophical Society. Awarded Pulitzer Prize for *A Further Range*.
1938	Death of Robert Frost's wife, Elinor.
1939	*Collected Poems* with additions published. Frost bought Homer Noble Farm in Ripton, Vermont.
1940	Death of Carol Frost by his own hand.
1942	*A Witness Tree* published.

1943	Frost awarded Pulitzer Prize for *A Witness Tree.* Made George Ticknor Fellow in Humanities, Dartmouth College.
1945	*A Masque of Reason* published.
1947	*Steeple Bush* and *A Masque of Mercy* published. Modern Library Edition of *The Poems of Robert Frost* published.
1949	Frost appointed Simpson Lecturer in Literature, Amherst College.
1950-1960	Resolution of the United States Senate recognized Frost on his seventy-fifth birthday in 1950. Received many other honors in the decade of the 1950's, including honorary degrees from Oxford University and Cambridge University. Became Consultant in Poetry, Library of Congress. Eighty-fifth birthday dinner given in New York City by his publishers, Henry Holt and Company, in 1960.
1961	Frost participated in inauguration of President John F. Kennedy. Read "The Gift Outright."
1962	Awarded Congressional Medal by President Kennedy. *In the Clearing* published.
1963	(January 29) Frost died in Boston.

1. Figures of a Poet

Lloyd N. Dendinger

Robert Frost: The Popular and the Central Poetic Images

Stephen Spender recently raised an old question about the relationship between the American poet and the American public:

> It is difficult for an English poet to understand that so many American poets seem to think of being a poet as the tragic vocation of a hero doomed to neglect, even when he plays out the drama of his being misunderstood before large university audiences. . . . But the death of Jarrell and of Roethke, the recurrent breakdowns of Robert Lowell and John Berryman, the fury of a poet as gifted as Shapiro at his colleagues who still write formal verse—all seem directly or indirectly the result of the extremely unhappy relationship of the American poet with an American public.[1]

This enigmatic, unhappy relationship has been of central concern in American letters since at least the death of Edgar Allan Poe,

From *American Quarterly,* XXI (Winter, 1969), 792-804. Published with the permission of the author and the Trustees of the University of Pennsylvania.
[1] "On English and American Poetry," *Saturday Review* (Apr. 23, 1966), p. 20.

and the English poet's difficulty in understanding it is shared by everyone who considers the matter. For it is of such fundamental cultural significance as to preclude explanations in terms of simple, one to one, cause and effect relationships. The Calvinist sanctification of work, the practical demands of a pioneer society, the profit motive of laissez-faire capitalism and the constant and frequently overwhelming challenges of providing just the material necessities of a dynamic, constantly expanding, urban-industrial society, all contribute to the uneasy self-consciousness of the man who decides to follow, in Hawthorne's terms, the "idle" profession of a writer. There is a kind of real continuity in American history to be found in the relationship between the problems of the struggle for existence in the frontier settlements of the 18th and 19th centuries and those raised by the severe civil strife of our major cities today. This land has always needed men of action to cut forests, clear and plow fields, build roads, bridges and cities, to put out fires and to rebuild again and again. In light of this continuity, the contempt in which Hawthorne imagined himself held by his ancestors still has its bite today:

> 'A writer of story-books! What kind of business in life,—what mode of glorifying God, or being serviceable to mankind in his day and generation—may that be? Why, the degenerate fellow might as well have been a fiddler!'[2]

The unhappy relationship between the modern American poet and an American public of which Stephen Spender speaks has deep roots. The popularity of Robert Frost is one of the most recent and illuminating chapters in its long history.

Frost's popularity is troublesome because it goes against the cherished concept that the American society is extremely hostile to the artist who insists upon questioning the practical, material values and aspirations of that society. This concept was given dramatic expression by Ezra Pound and his generation; Pound was to emphasize, with glee one suspects, that Frost had to leave America to get recognition. Sinclair Lewis' Babbitt and H. L. Mencken's "boobocracy" are even less subtle reflections of the attitude of that period. But the roots of the concept go much deeper, finding overt expression at least as early as Hawthorne's self-conscious reflections in "The Custom House."

---

[2] "The Custom-House": Introductory to *The Scarlet Letter*.

From Emerson's 1837 *American Scholar* address to the end of the century, American literature is characterized by a defensive self-consciousness never far beneath the surface but most obvious in Whitman's "barbaric yawp," Mark Twain's burlesques of European traditions and Henry James' admission that he was "that strange monster, an artist."[3] James' expatriation set the pattern for Pound's generation in which the self-consciousness became defiance, and the solution was sought in flight to less hostile environments. Frost in this respect as in most others did not conform to the pattern of his contemporaries. He spent two years in England, writing about *New* England; he was never one of the expatriates. His rebellion, his "lover's quarrel" was "with the world" in general and never exclusively with his native land. Nevertheless, the persistent attention paid Frost's popularity and the accompanying determination to explain it away (i.e., Frost is popular because he is not a first-rate poet, *or* he is popular because his readers don't understand him) arise naturally out of the old concern about the irresistible leveling tendencies of modern peoples, out of a fundamental lack of faith in the culture of a democracy. Frost's career is, therefore, among other things, a valuable chapter in our continuing efforts to define the artist's role in the democratic society of modern America.

A consistent pattern in the critical responses to Frost's poetry from 1913 to the present has developed out of the regularity with which the various commentators have distinguished between the Frost they are praising as a significant modern poet and the "popular" Frost. Time after time the point is made that the poet's popularity rests upon a general misunderstanding of his poetry and that the poet's true merits arise from subtleties too fine and profundities too deep for all but a highly favored few. One basis of this attitude is implicit in an early evaluation by Ezra Pound, who although he found Frost "vurry Amur'kn" believed nevertheless that he had at least "the seeds of grace."[4] A more recent and a more explicit expression of this consistent duality occurred in 1959, in what has been called the "Trilling-Adams episode."

In the summer of 1959 Lionel Trilling published an essay in the *Partisan Review* entitled "A Speech on Robert Frost: A Cultural

[3] Letter to Henry Adams, Mar. 21, 1914. See *The Letters of Henry James,* ed. Percy Lubbock (New York, 1920), II, 361.
[4] Quoted by Elizabeth Shepley Sergeant in *Robert Frost: The Trial By Existence* (New York, 1960), p. 103.

10   *Robert Frost: The Popular and the Central Poetic Images*

Episode."[5] As the title indicates, the body of the piece is a speech
Trilling gave at a birthday dinner honoring Frost on his eighty-
fifth birthday which he felt should be published because, as he
puts it, the speech was the "occasion for a disturbance of some
magnitude."[6] Various and forceful exceptions were taken to some
of the observations on Frost and his career, the focus of which was
on the distinction between the Frost Trilling admired and the
Frost he perceived "existing in the minds of some of his admirers."[7]
The theme of the speech and the focal point of the attacks upon
it is that there are "two" Robert Frosts, the widely and tradition-
ally admired rural American poet who "reassures us by his affirmations of old virtues, simplicities, pieties, and ways of feeling" and
Trilling's "terrifying poet" who, like Sophocles, made plain to his
people "the terrible things of human life."

The principal attack upon this point of view which was to begin
the "disturbance of some magnitude" was that made by J. Donald
Adams in the April 12 New York *Times* Book Review. After classifying Frost as "pre-eminently" of that company of "writers who
are indubitably American," Adams identifies what he considers the
basic cause of Trilling's diffidence on the occasion of the birthday
speech:

> His difficulty was that although—or perhaps I should say because
> —he is a native New Yorker, he showed little understanding of the
> United States. That circumstance has not, however, prevented
> other sons of this city from grasping more fully the meaning of
> the American experience. Professor Trilling's failure to do so is,
> indeed, one widely shared by other American intellectuals.[8]

This difficulty, according to Adams, led Trilling to find the "key to
the understanding of his Frost in D. H. Lawrence's criticism of
American literature," whereas if he had read Emerson instead, "he
might have lost *his* Frost and discovered the one he turns his back
on, for a goodly part of Frost the man and Frost the poet is
rooted . . . in Emerson, who was his intellectual and spiritual
godfather." Adams feels that Trilling, like Lawrence before him,
has become "lost in the Freudian wood," and he takes strong
exception to calling Frost a terrifying poet, claiming for Frost a

[5] XXVI (Summer 1959), 445-52.
[6] *Ibid.*, p. 445.
[7] *Ibid.*, p. 450.
[8] "Speaking of Books," Apr. 12, 1959, p. 2.

poise which precludes terror, a "private air-conditioning system [which] he got . . . from Emerson." He concludes his remarks with the following observation:

> All this country needs is to recapture its earlier vision. One of the silliest remarks ever made about the American experience came from one of the editors of your favorite magazine, the *Partisan Review*. Mr. William Phillips solemnly observed that American literature has played hide-and-seek with American experience for lack of 'an image, or cluster of images, of the national experience available to literature.' No such lack exists, and both of you should re-read one of the great American poems. It is by Robert Frost, and it is called "The Gift Outright."

The third phase of this cultural tempest, this "disturbance of some magnitude," came in the form of letters published in the May 3rd issue of the Book Review applauding Adams for his attack upon the birthday speech.[9] There were nine of these letters, the writers of which included the editor of *Atlantic Monthly*, the publisher of *Saturday Review*, two poets and a literary scholar. Trilling says that he was "surprised by the low personal and intellectual tone of these letters," all of which "sounded a note of bitterness, or of personal grievance, or of triumph over my having been so thoroughly taken down by Mr. Adams."[10] The following excerpts from the letters used by Trilling to illustrate his point fairly represent the prevailing tone:

> 'Frost might have had the Nobel Prize if so many New York critics hadn't gone whoring after European gods.' 'This Trilling fella had it coming to him for some time.' 'I hope Robert Frost was having a nice plate of buckwheat cakes and Vermont maple syrup as he read Mr. Adams's remarks. He couldn't have done better unless he had taken the so-called professor out to the woodshed.' 'I am a Freudian psychoanalyst, but I couldn't agree with Mr. Adams more. Imagine calling Frost a terrifying poet.'[11]

Trilling feels that his speech, Adams' attack upon it and the letters applauding the attack all constitute an "episode" which "will yield cultural conclusions to whoever wants to draw them."[12]

---

[9] May 3, 1959, p. 24.
[10] Trilling, p. 446.
[11] *Ibid.*
[12] *Ibid.*, p. 447.

Frost's popularity may be defined in a number of ways, the most obvious and least disputable being in terms of honors and awards, national and international public appearances, and the sale of his books, which probably totals something near to half a million volumes. The basis of this popularity is usually ascribed to his subject matter, to the "sense of directness" which his natural diction and logical structure give the poetry, and to his "platform personality." There is no basis for quarreling with the facts and figures of the definition in the first place, and little if any basis for quarreling with those factors thought to be responsible for the popularity. But there is a serious gap in our knowledge between that description of the poetry and the man which accounts for his popular reputation and the generally unquestioned assumption that most of his "popular" audience just naturally do not understand him. There has been much talk about a "mythical Robert Frost" existing in the minds of the American people. Attention needs to be called to the fact that in order to sustain the first myth, the creation of a second has been made necessary, for it has been necessary for those who object most strenuously to the popular Frost to make some broad assumptions about the popular audience which is defined over and over again as those readers who do not understand the poet. For although there is little or no evidence to indicate what the popular audience—by definition, in the area of poetry, an anonymous, silent audience—thinks and feels, the central thesis of the criticism and appraisals of Frost from 1913 on has been that his popularity is based on a lack of understanding. What emerges from this central concern is a definition of a "popular" American mind and by implication a definition, generally denigratory, of American culture. Implicit in the critical record of Frost's reputation is an answer to Tocqueville's question about the irresistible leveling tendencies of democratic societies: and the answer is that the leveling tendencies have been made manifest; that the "popular" American mind is the central index to the resulting cultural poverty; and that any artist popular with an audience made up of such minds must be suspect and is almost surely of not more than second-rate significance. Hence, Frost's popularity must either be explained away or used against him.

An illustrative consideration of this problem for "popular" consumption appeared in a cover story on Frost in *Time* magazine in 1950, in which, in a typical stroke, *Time* manages simultaneously to insult and applaud the "U.S. readers." After making the point that "Vermonters find nothing outlandish or alarming about Robert Frost," the article makes the following appraisal:

Neither do U.S. readers, to most of whom the word "poet" still carries a faint suggestion of pale hands, purple passions and flowing ties. They understand what he writes—or understand enough of it to like what they understand. They find his dialogue poems as invigorating as a good argument, his lyrics as engaging, sometimes as magical, as Mother Goose. In a literary age so preoccupied with self-expression that it sometimes seems intent on making the reader feel stupid, Robert Frost has won him by treating him as an equal.

In short, Robert Frost is a popular poet.[13]

Obviously, except for the last line quoted, nothing in the appraisal is or can be supported by any kind of evidence. But as delightfully imaginative and as wholly indefensible as the "pale hands, purple passions and flowing ties" are, the piece is valuable because its insubstantiality is representative of much that has been said on the subject.

The formal criticism is, to be sure, characterized by greater care in the matter of defining the popular audience than is the *Time* article. John Ciardi, writing for the commemorative issue of *Saturday Review* in 1963, visualizes a possible popular image, strikes the familiar chord about distortion, but also points to a source of that distortion:

Let me yet hope that no man, for sentimental reasons, will be moved to eulogize the confectionary image of a kindly, vague, white-haired great-grandfather when there is the reality of a magnificently passionate man to honor. . . .

He was our best. And certainly to honor him in the truth of himself is a least homage. Yet the sentimental distortion remains fixed in the public mind, and has marred every public recognition tendered him from honorable sentiment but in the blindness of sentimentality.[14]

M. L. Rosenthal, writing in response to the Trilling-Adams episode of 1959, attributes the popular image to the "publicists," who "turned him into the sagacious and humorous country-poet Mr. Adams loves . . . one variant of that grand archetype the Good Grey Poet into which they have relegated Whitman and Sandburg. . . ."[15] Singling out the publicists and the phraseology of occasions of public recognition moves in the right direction of

[13] "Pawky Poet," Oct. 9, 1950, p. 76.
[14] "Robert Frost: To Earthward," Feb. 23, 1963, p. 24.
[15] "The Robert Frost Controversy," *Nation,* CLXXXVIII (June 20, 1959), 560.

specifying what one means by popular image. But the fanfare of publicists and the obviously ceremonious language of public occasion are hardly taken seriously enough to account for the scope and depth of the concern over Frost's popularity.

Yvor Winters, Robert Langbaum and George W. Nitchie all probe deeper into the relationship between Frost as poet and Frost as public figure. For Winters, there is a real and unhappy relationship between the two. As he sees it, "Frost's confusion is similar to that of the public, and most readers of poetry still regard poetry as a vague emotional indulgence: they do not take poetry seriously and they dislike serious poetry." And Winters is perhaps the most explicit commentator of all when it comes to specifying the causes of the confusion at the basis of Frost's popularity:

> The principles which have hampered Frost's development, the principles of Emersonian and Thoreauistic Romanticism, are the principles which he has openly espoused, and they are widespread in our culture. Until we understand these last and the dangers inherent in them and so abandon them in favor of better, we are unlikely to produce many poets greater than Frost, although a few poets may have intelligence enough to work clear of such influences; and we are likely to deteriorate more or less rapidly both as individuals and as a nation.[16]

Langbaum and Nitchie both speak on the subject in a manner much in common with Winters, though neither sees the matter as darkly as he does. For Langbaum, Frost's poetry "delivers us from the poignancy of the historical moment to place us in contact with a survival-making eternal folk wisdom. We can live by Frost's poetry as we could not by Yeats' or Pound's."[17] Nitchie's summary is characterized by the same kind of explicit thoroughness as is Winters':

> Frost is important as a kind of American culture hero, as an index of certain persistent American characteristics. Discussing V. L. Parrington, Lionel Trilling has aptly characterized this aspect of Frost. Parrington's 'best virtue was real and important. . . . He knew what so many literary historians do not know, that emotions

---

[16] "Robert Frost: or, The Spiritual Drifter as Poet," in *Robert Frost: A Collection of Critical Essays* (Englewood Cliffs, N.J., 1962), pp. 81-82.
[17] Langbaum, "The New Nature Poetry," *American Scholar,* XXVIII (Summer 1959), 330.

and ideas are the sparks that fly when the mind meets difficulties.'
Like Parrington, and like the perhaps mythical representative
American, Frost 'admires will in the degree that he suspects mind.'
Like Parrington, Frost 'still stands at the center of American
thought about American culture because . . . he expresses the
chronic American belief that there exists an opposition between
reality and mind and that one must enlist oneself in the party
of reality.'[18]

All three of these men have serious misgiving about the cultural
ramifications of Frost's affinities with his public, but they do not
resort to the quite common procedure of explaining away the
popularity on the basis of a lack of understanding. For Winters,
to be sure, there is misunderstanding, but it is a mutual affair;
both Frost *and* his public are confused. For Langbaum and Nitchie,
the affinities are real, but at the subrational level of folk wisdom
and cultural hero worship.[19] There is the implication in the latter
two of the attitude made explicit by Winters that Frost's popularity is the result of something other than positive, desirable cultural conditions. That is, the position here is not that Frost's
public is incapable of understanding him, but that, alas, they
"understand," in the sense that they respond to those very values
the poet would have them respond to, all too well. Frost's popularity is not explained away; it is, in a very real sense, used against
him and in a critical assault upon those peculiarly American traits
of mind from which it springs. Consideration of this assault leads
us back again to our early point of setting forth, the Trilling-
Adams episode of 1959.

The duality of the Trilling-Adams episode is representative of
the duality running through the criticism of Frost's poetry since
Ezra Pound's observation that Frost is "vurry Amur'kn" with at
least "the seeds of grace." And it is a duality which has its roots
in the 19th century literary concern for a definable American
culture distinct from its European sources. For when Adams and
his supporters object to what should be considered high praise, the
favorable comparison of Frost with Sophocles, what they are really
objecting to is the reinterpretation of the poet in the broad terms

[18] *Human Values in the Poetry of Robert Frost* (Durham, N.C., 1960),
pp. 220-21.
[19] Langbaum calls attention to Reginald Cook's use in *The Dimensions of
Robert Frost* of the term "sabiduria" to denote the kind of folk wisdom
Frost gives expression to.

of western culture as opposed to his reputation as an unmistakably American, and even more specifically, a New England poet. Trilling, much like Winters and Nitchie, sees the popularity of Frost negatively as a reflection of a regrettable definition of American culture in rural terms. Winters' "Emersonian-Thoreauistic Romanticism," Nitchie's "opposition between reality and mind," and Trilling's manifestly "rural" America are all aspects of the same definition of American culture, of that definition which places great emphasis upon the physical importance of the new continent and upon the challenge of the wilderness in the shaping of that culture. And all three men are wholly or partially rejecting that definition as the most important one; for them, the values of American culture are the values of western European culture—for Winters, "the principles of Greek and Christian thought," for Trilling, urban, cosmopolitan culture—and America in the most important sense is not a new culture at all but rather an extension of the old into a new environment. It is this concept which J. Donald Adams, who considers "The Gift Outright" one of Frost's great poems, rejects in protesting Trilling's enlargement of the poet's achievement to the stature of Sophoclean tragedy. For Adams, Frost is an Emersonian poet, a poet of the *new* land and the *new* vision, the answer to Emerson's plea for "the timely man, the new religion, the reconciler, whom all things await."[20]

Trilling called his speech and the responses it evoked a "cultural episode," and the cultural significance of the episode is that, serving as a kind of microcosmic summary of much of the criticism of Frost's poetry, it involves not only an appraisal of Robert Frost the poet, but also various definitions of the culture which he represents. Trilling and Adams stand at opposite poles in their respective estimations of the central nature of Frost's achievement, and read selectively, the poetry provides considerable support for both views, neither of which accounts, however, for the vital center of the vision making possible the extremes. Frost is more optimistic than pessimistic, more affirmative than negative, and in this respect Adams is closer to the truth of the matter than is Trilling. But the two poetic postures central to Frost's achievement, that of the realistic regionalist and that of the traveler of "Stopping by Woods on a Snowy Evening," raise images other than those used

---

[20] *The Poet.* First published in *Essays,* Second Series, 1844. Quotations are from *Selected Prose and Poetry,* ed. Reginald L. Cook (2nd ed., New York, 1969).

by Trilling and Adams and define Frost's affinities with his "public," the basis of any meaningful popularity, as a synthesis of the old and the new, of the inherited, antithetical traditions of romanticism and naturalism. This synthesis is responsible for a poetic vision distinctly modern and even more distinctly American. Whether poetry can indeed be written about "anything" and from any point of view is, to say the least, highly debatable. Matthew Arnold pointed out in *Culture and Anarchy* that "the great works by which . . . the human spirit has manifested its approaches to totality and to a full, harmonious perfection . . . come, not from Nonconformists, but from men who either belong to Establishments or have been trained in them." The point is as vital today as it ever was in evaluations of poetic achievement. Frost neither belonged to the Establishments nor was he trained in them, and it is because of this very fact that he is most distinctly a modern American poet, for modern America has a distinct, definable culture primarily based on its continuing attempts to free itself from the "Establishments." Whether the best poetry can be written in such an environment without the kinds of adjustments made, for example, by Eliot and Wallace Stevens is also a matter for debate, although not the issue here. The point here is that Frost is indeed very American, in part because of his faithful portrayal of New England character and the New England countryside, but more importantly because of his American frame of mind, because of his refusal to subordinate experience to abstract, systematic thought. For him, as for Hawthorne, Melville, Howells and James, in particular, before him, "reality" was characterized before all else by a dynamic, vital ambiguity which would allow itself to be bound to no thesis.

Robert Frost's popularity can be explained in terms of his personality, his "platform" personality more particularly; in terms of his poetry and in terms of the cultural conditions responsible for making the matter such a significant one. I have not been concerned in this study with the first of these factors, primarily because discussions of successful platform personalities, of effective, dramatic speakers, of showmen, always turn ultimately on quasi-mystical explanations involving indefinable qualities responsible for the magic rapport between speaker and audience. Frost's physical appearance, his voice, his wit and his sense of timing, all made him the popular success he was on the lecture platform. But no one who has ever heard or seen him read will be satisfied with this or any other explanation of the appeal. This is not to praise him too highly; indeed, many will consider it hardly praise at all to call his appeal that of the successful showman, but that is largely what it was. The fact that his poetry was his script made it, to be sure, a special kind of entertainment, but the poet was too easily lost—as he frequently is whether he is a talented reader or not—to the platform personality. Frost could conceivably have made a name for himself reading someone else's poetry, so separate and distinct are the talents of reading and writing. But he blurred the line between the two since he was reading his own poetry, and one of the various popular images of the poet is that of the kindly but sharp-witted old man, pausing for the laughter sure to come, or finally, fumbling in the bright sunlight and an irreverent breeze with a scrap of paper on a presidential inaugural platform.

Frost's platform personality, his public "mask," might well have been developed with little or no relationship to his poetry. But there is a significant relationship between the two suggested by the poetic mask of the New England sage who makes his appearance in "Brown's Descent" and who becomes increasingly conspicuous from that point on. This is the mask of "New Hampshire" and of the political and scientific satires of the 1930s and 1940s in particular. The public mask and this poetic mask are practically identical. Reading "Brown's Descent," "New Hampshire" and from the last book, *In The Clearing,* "Some Science Fiction" is very much like seeing and hearing Frost himself performing, creating the public mask, so closely related to its counterpart in the poetry. So it is possible to speak of a second popular image which has its roots in the poetry itself and which is practically indistinguishable except for that fact from the public, platform mask.

There are at least two more definable images in the poetry itself which bear upon the explanation of Frost's popularity and they began developing earlier than either of the two masks above. The first image is that of the realistic regionalist of *North of Boston,* and this image, which does not qualify for the terms "mask" or "persona," is of fundamental importance to Frost's early popularity with his peers, with Ezra Pound and Amy Lowell in particular. This is one of the most specific of the images because so many of the early reviewers and critics focused upon it as the poet's distinguishing characteristic. One can say with assurance that Frost's early popularity depended in very large part upon the image defined by the critics in response to *North of Boston.* Frost was pictured time after time as the grim realist, extending to verse the traditions and techniques of the prose realists. This is the most narrowly defined image of all, standing at the far extreme from the wise, patriarchal figure reciting from the presidential inaugural platform. And the narrowly defined image is the more precise of the two: the record is clear and sure about the virtues of the realistic regionalist; what Frost meant to the much larger audience who heard him recite "The Gift Outright" in 1961 is far from being precisely defined, if indeed it is definable at all.

Frost's central poetic character is that of the traveler through the natural world, and this character began taking shape even before the development of the realistic posture of *North of Boston*, in the nature poetry of *A Boy's Will*. The traveler does not mature in that first volume; one of the important influences upon his development was the realistic posture developed at first independently in *North of Boston*. The traveler in "The Wood-Pile" and "After Apple-Picking" is the traveler of *A Boy's Will*, but the traveler seasoned, much more cautious, much more determined to hold himself objectively aloof in his evaluations of experience. He is much more the realist except that he does respond subjectively in the poems; we are aware of his presence, and of his determination to maintain control of the relationship he sees existing between himself and the natural world around him. The traveler comes to full maturity in "Stopping by Woods on a Snowy Evening" where we see him bring to a full synthesis the "constructive and destructive" forces of the natural world that is both outside of him and in his own human nature. This synthesis, this control, is central to Frost's poetic achievement and to his popularity. It makes possible that interpretation of his poetry to which Trilling and so many other critics have objected, that interpretation which completely robs the poetry of its terror, of its vision of evil, of its most modern sense of nausea at the perception of the infinite reaches of space, of the "empty spaces/Between stars—on stars where no human race is." The image of the traveler from this point of view augments the image of the public mask, of the kindly platform personality. He is from this point of view a descriptive nature poet who calmly surveys and sweetly portrays an innocent pastoral world.

Such a view does not, of course, do justice to the traveler's vision. Nor does it provide a very meaningful definition of Frost's popularity except in a negative way. That is, if Frost's central poetic character is as widely misunderstood as so many would have it, then his popularity is a result not of his poetry but of the limitations of his audience, a measurement not of his achievement but of the cultural poverty of his environment. The popular audience from this point of view is necessarily an inferior audience not capable of nor really interested in understanding the poet. The focus of this study has not been to take issue with this point of view, but rather to examine the basis of it. Neither Frost's poetry nor the record of the criticism of that poetry provides a satisfactory explanation of the cultural episode that began with Ezra Pound's emphasis upon Frost's early failure to gain recognition at home and received the relatively late re-emphasis shortly before Frost's death in the debate between Lionel Trilling and J. Donald Adams. That cultural episode, that persistent preoccupation not so much with the poetry as with the poet's popularity, is best explained by the uses to which the popularity can so conveniently be put in the continuing debate about the quality of the mass culture of a democratic state. Frost's most ardent admirers have felt compelled to explain away his popularity by saying that he is simply not understood by his popular audience; one of his most perceptive critics, Yvor Winters, has seen the matter rather as the result of a confusion "widespread in our culture."

In the final analysis, it is explanations like those of Winters and Nitchie that are most meaningful in an attempt to understand the cultural phenomenon of Frost's popularity. This is not to say that theirs are the best or that they are even wholly valid explanations, but rather that the most meaningful approach is the one which they take of attempting to explain the basis of the appeal which the poetry has for the popular audience instead of trying to explain away that appeal as a result of widespread misunderstanding. And one of the best explanations of the basis of that appeal can be made by the central image in the poetry, which is of Frost's principal poetic character, the traveler through the natural world.

I have considered elsewhere certain affinities between the traveler as he appears in "Stopping by Woods on a Snowy Evening" and Thoreau in the posture he assumes in *Walden* and Nick Adams in *Big Two-Hearted River*.[21] If Frost's popularity is to be explained positively rather than negatively, it can best be explained by the central image of the poetry which has so much in common with that recurrent and most popular image in American literature, the solitary man confronting the natural world, usually the great

---

[21] "The Irrational Appeal of Frost's Dark, Deep Woods," *Southern Review*, II (Autumn 1966), 822-29.

American wilderness. Frost's traveler is very American in the sense that Leatherstocking is very American; and in the sense that Ishmael, Hester Prynne, Thoreau as he appears in *Walden*, Huck Finn and Nick Adams are very American. All of these but Ishmael have in common their confrontation with the American wilderness which has been the most important symbol at both the literary and legendary levels of the principal challenge of the American experiment, the breaking with the traditions of the past. The central question has been whether or not civilized man could realize the potentialities of the new Eden, if he could indeed break with the human condition as it had been defined by more than two thousand years of western civilization and begin truly anew in the new world. That the answer to the question is so obviously no does not make the question any less important to an understanding of American culture. Indeed, the very men responsible for articulating the question repeatedly said no to it themselves: civilization overtakes Leatherstocking; Hester stays in Boston; Huck's final desperate cry pales into insignificance against his repeated failures to escape; Frost's traveler turns away from the woods. But the hope of moral rejuvenation has been hard to give up and there is still faith in man's ability to wrest it physically from the natural environment. And the man to do this is the practical, simple man close to nature, the man who knows about birch trees, axe-helves, rock walls, pasture lands and snowstorms. This is the man who strides through Frost's poetry—he is more American than New England, and he is responsible more than any other factor for Frost's appeal. As there is a merging of the public platform mask with the poetic mask of the New England sage, so there is a merging of the personality of Frost the man in still another role of his, that of the simple, plainspoken farmer, with the poetic mask of the traveler through the natural world. And it is the combination of these final two which is responsible for the most significantly popular image of the poet.

James M. Cox

Robert Frost and the Edge of the Clearing

When Robert Frost nears a university campus in this country there is a bustle of interest and activity extending beyond the confining borders of the English department. A curious observer is struck by the realization that Frost's approaching appearance is no mere item on the college calendar but an event which makes its presence felt in the area of public relations. Even the distant administrative machinery can be heard to stir in anticipation of Frost's arrival, and when the hour comes round for Frost himself to take the stage a member of officialdom above and beyond the orbit of mere liberal arts is likely to perform the rites of introduction as the Frost cycle begins over again. It has been a cycle repeated in one place or another for almost thirty years, expanding with the passage of time as Frost has established himself securely in the position which Mark Twain created in the closing years of the last century—the position of American literary man as public entertainer. Frost brings to his rôle the grave face, the regional turn of phrase, the pithy generalization, and the salty experience

From *The Virginia Quarterly Review,* XXXV (Winter, 1959), 73-88. Published with the permission of the author.

which Twain before him brought to his listeners. He is the homespun farmer who assures his audiences that he was made in America before the advent of the assembly line, and he presides over his following with what is at once casual ease and lonely austerity.

Because the popularity surrounding Frost the public figure and hovering about his poetry has become the halo under which admirers enshrine his work, to many serious critics bent on assessing the value of the poetry this halo becomes a sinister mist clouding the genuine achievement. Malcolm Cowley, for example, has raised a dissenting voice against the foggy approval; and even Randall Jarrell, who has written some of the most sensitive appraisals of Frost's poetry, inclines to dissociate the real or "other" Frost from the brassy New England character who parades before his audiences as what Jarrell calls "The Only Genuine Robert Frost in Captivity."

Yet Frost's success as a public figure, rather than being a calculated addition to his poetic career, is a natural extension of it, and one way to approach his poetry is to see that the character who moves in the poems anticipates the one who occupies the platform. They are in all essentials the same character—a dramatization of the farmer poet come out of his New England landscape bringing with him the poems he plays a rôle in. To observe this insistent regional stance is to realize that Frost has done, and is still doing, for American poetry what Faulkner has more recently accomplished in American fiction. They both have made their worlds in the image of their particular regions, and, moving within these self-contained and self-made microcosms, they have given their provincial centers universal significance. But while Faulkner has concerned himself with establishing the legendary Yoknapatawpha county and its mythical components, Frost has, from the very first poem of "A Boy's Will," been engaged in creating the myth of Robert Frost, The Only Genuine Robert Frost in Captivity. It is a myth with a hero and a drama.

The hero is the New England farmer who wears the mask, or better, the anti-mask of the traditional poet. But it is not a literal mask concealing the poet who lurks behind it; rather, it is a mode of being which releases the poetic personality in the person of a character who lives and moves. Whatever duality we may wish to ascribe between mask and man is actually present in the mask itself, for the mask—or character—of Frost is finally more real than any hypothetical Frost we may envision behind the scenes. The very life of the character depends upon his creator's ability to project his whole personality into the image he assumes. Frost is, for his audience, a "character" simply because he represents both in language and outlóok a vastly familiar figure to them, a kind of traditional stage Yankee full of gnomic wisdom and prankish humor, carrying his history in his head and venturing cryptic comment upon all experience in a sufficiently provincial manner to remind them of a preconceived caricature.

It is Frost's ability to *be* a farmer poet which distinguishes him most sharply from Wordsworth, with whom he is often compared. Wordsworth played the part of the Poet concerned with common man, but Frost has persistently cast himself in the rôle of the common man concerned with poetry. Such a strategy, while it cuts him off from the philosophically autobiographical poetry which Wordsworth built toward, opens up avenues of irony, wit, comedy, and dramatic narrative largely closed to Wordsworth. For the poetic ego, held in objectivity by the anti-mask which both releases and contains it, is exposed to a control and ironic self-awareness foreign to the serious and subjective Wordsworth, who, although he felt keenly the joy of experience, rarely descended to humor.

Thus, instead of direct revelation through autobiography and confession, Frost has from the start pursued the more indirect but equally effective mode of dramatizing and characterizing himself. Even the lyrics of "A Boy's Will" lean toward narrative and monologue, and the peculiar Frost idiom, so integral a part of the Frost character who eventually emerges, is evident in remarkable maturity in such early poems as "Into My Own," "Mowing," "A Tuft of Flowers," and "In Hardwood Groves." The dramatic monologues and dialogues of "North of Boston," which have impressed many critics as a wide departure from Frost's lyric vein, constitute a full discovery and perfection of that idiom. Moreover, Frost himself emerges prominently as a member of the volume's *dramatis personae*, playing an important rôle in nine of the sixteen poems. As a matter of fact, "Mending Wall," the first poem in the volume, marks the full-dress entrance of the farmer poet. Possessed of all the characteristics by which we have come to know him, this figure is full of sly observations as he assumes a slightly comic poise with eye asquint—already poetry is "his kind of fooling." He goes to great length to disarm his audience with colloquial familiarity and whimsical parentheses. Then, after an agile imaginative leap in the grand style, he returns to earth as if he feared being caught off guard.

This cautious refusal to declaim too far or too soon, while it may leave too much unsaid or enclose the issue in a blurred dual vision which accepts both sides, is often one of Frost's most effective modes of self awareness. Thus, when Yvor Winters, in his discussion of "The Road Not Taken," holds Frost responsible for refusing to make clear the kind of choice represented by the two roads which "diverged in a yellow wood," he misses the comic criticism the speaker is directing against himself. As Professor Ben W. Griffith has rightly observed, Frost is indulging in a bemused self-portrayal. When he made the choice, he made it not profoundly but tentatively and uncertainly; he was even incapable of distinguishing which road *was* the least traveled—"And both that morning equally lay/In leaves no step had trodden black"—but he envisions the day when he shall sighingly, and rather heavily, tell of his decision to take the road "less traveled by," the road that has made "all the difference." The poem, in addition to demolishing the cliché of life's crossroads, is a vision of as well as a warning against the wise old farmer poet whose retrospective summary of his past may attribute a wisdom to former actions which was never there.

Beyond this playfully ironic self-portrayal so characteristic of Frost, there is also the tragic self-awareness which enabled him to create the great dramatic monologues. In such poems as "The Fear," "Home Burial," and "A Servant to Servants," for example, sensitive wives are so caught between the lonely natural world and the rigid proverbs of their husbands that, locked in an unutterable loneliness, they disintegrate into hysteria or slump into depression. Those husbands bear enough similarity to the figure of the farmer poet to indicate how much Frost realizes, for all his willingness to exploit the poetic possibilities of aphorism—how blind and hard a proverb quoter can be.

If Frost needs self-awareness to protect himself from the Yankee wisdom in which he specializes, he also needs it to confront the world he moves in, that lonely and desolate world where the Frost drama is staged. Despite his literal realism, Frost has never been a mere reflector of his chosen New England locale; rather, he has managed to create the illusion of making the world he describes, and in his hands the region north of Boston becomes a self-sustaining yet surprisingly inclusive microcosm with the character of Frost himself at its center. Even the eccentricities of crabbed New England speech and attitude have poetic validity because, more than being details to characterize and individuate a geographical province, they belong to the central character and constitute his authentic signature upon the world he makes and owns. The entire region beneath his vision becomes his property, an extension of himself, and Frost's ability to project his character into his provincial world has given his poetry the double thrust it so often possesses—a thrust outward into the wild nature in which he persistently finds himself, and a thrust inward to the darker regions of the self.

Like his great New England antecedents, Emerson and Thoreau, he casts his own shadow upon the landscape he surveys. Skeptical in his cast of mind, Frost inclines away from their tendency to abstract doctrine, but he retains much of the method and many of the attitudes they left behind them, nor is it surprising that "Walden" is one of his favorite books. Thoreau's strategy was to move round and round the pond, keeping his eye alertly upon that self-contained body of water until, in the final chapter of his microcosmic odyssey, he had possessed it. His progress was parabolic in the mathematical sense, for his walking arc was midway between the pond, the focus, and the set of principles which formed the directrix of his journey. The more Thoreau discovered about the pond, the more he plotted a central index to life, since the pond was both mirror for man and eye of God in which the traveler could take a final measure of himself. In sounding it he sounded himself, and Thoreau fulfilled his dual rôle of explorer and surveyor by at once discovering and charting a course to sustain him through all modes of existence.

Frost has also been intent on possessing his world, but he started with no given center, no sure assumptions, and no assurance that there would be assumptions. His work has been no experiment to test himself, but the venture of a lifetime. His first poem in *A Boy's Will*, significantly entitled "Into My Own," expressed a wish that the deep woods confronting him, instead of being a mere mask of darkness, stretched endlessly out toward the edge of doom. Doubling his subjunctive, Frost wished that he could lose himself in the infinite depths of such a forest, but extended a subdued invitation to those who loved him to follow his footsteps into the trackless wood. Although Frost's title of this first volume of poetry came from Longfellow's memorable refrain, "A boy's will is the wind's will," he was already advancing into the areas where Longfellow had refused to go. For in "My Lost Youth," Longfellow, after quite brilliantly returning into the Portland of his memory toward the secret regions of his boyhood, had paused at the threshold of Deering's Woods as if confronting a secret terror and, content to excuse himself with a pious admonition— "There are things of which I may not speak"—, he retreated back into nostalgia. Taking and retaining the boy's will to explore, Frost has forced a clearing in the woods which Longfellow declined to enter, and his career has been in many ways a realization of his earliest wish.

The clearing he has wrought is his own, and he works constantly at its edge, laying claim to the marginal world between the wild and the tame. The figure of the clearing, while it obviously does not appear in every poem, suggests the quality of experience which Frost has been intent upon possessing, and in "The Last Mowing," one of his most delicate lyrics, the dimensions as well as the drama of his world appear in sharp focus:

> There's a place called Far-away Meadow
> We never shall mow in again,
> Or such is the talk at the farmhouse:
> The meadow is finished with men.
> Then now is the chance for the flowers
> That can't stand mowers and plowers.
> It must be now, though, in season
> Before the not mowing brings trees on,
> Before trees, seeing the opening,
> March into a shadowy claim.
> The trees are all I'm afraid of,
> That flowers can't bloom in the shade of;
> It's no more men I'm afraid of;
> The meadow is done with the tame.
> The place for the moment is ours
> For you, O tumultuous flowers,
> To go to waste and go wild in,
> All shapes and colors of flowers,
> I needn't call you by name.

Remaining in the moving margin where resurgent nature returns upon abandoned meadowland, Frost attempts to wrest the moment of beauty elapsing where order dissolves into chaos. He is no more afraid of the threatening woods than at another time he has been afraid of the men who cleared the field, for the wild flowers perish before both forces. In the face of the oncoming woods, Frost discovers a moment of joy in the midst of his tender elegy, since in that forgotten territory he can perform a solitary celebration for the beauty which remains.

Seeing the nature of his task, one can understand why he con-
tended in "The Constant Symbol" that every poem is "an epitome
of the great predicament; a figure of the will braving alien entanglements." Indeed, the woods, always ready to encroach upon his
tenuous margin, suggest the alien entanglements against which
Frost pits his will, and the drama he sees the poet playing recalls
Emerson's insistence that a man must be self-reliant, "obeying the
Almighty Effort and advancing on Chaos and the dark." But even
as he accepts the antagonists of the Emersonian drama, Frost,
lacking Emerson's evangelical temperament, recognizes a larger
chaos and sees the drama of existence as man's willingness to risk
himself before the spell of the dark woods. For him self-reliance
becomes self-possession, and the victory lies not in the march
forward into the wilderness but in the freedom he feels while
patroling the boundary of consciousness. He accepts with almost
joy the entanglements because he knows that the material of the
unwrought poem inheres in that wilderness. Thus in "Pertinax"
he advocates holding on:

> Let Chaos storm!
> Let cloud shapes swarm!
> I wait for form.

And in "The Figure a Poem Makes," he is even more emphatic:
"All I would keep for myself is the freedom of my material—the
condition of body and mind to summons aptly now and then from
the vast chaos I have lived through."

Cryptic though his prose is, it is his own guarded commentary
upon his work, offering essential insights into his poetic terrain.
When Frost says that chaos lies behind him, he points up the
temporal dimension of his world. Unlike Emerson, he is deeply
concerned with his past—not the past of organized tradition so
much as the disorganized past he himself has strewn behind. The
literal facts of his New England world afford a scenic analogy
against which the Frost character performs his act, for the woods
he works in are no virgin wilderness but second-growth timber
come back to claim abandoned human landscape. The black cottage, the belilaced cellar hole "slowly closing like a dent in dough,"
the overgrown path, the old barn at the bottom of the fogs remain
forsakenly within his rural scenes as the surviving witnesses of
lost encounters with the forest. In repossessing them, Frost is turning back upon himself to reclaim the fragments of his personal

past—fragments which apparently meant nothing when they were current but which come to constitute the primary medium of exchange in the economy of reorganization.

Frugal as Frost's economy is, its aim is no easy security, for his clearing is as hard to hold as it is to win. In addition to the remnants of abandoned farms, there are also the living victims who linger in stunned confusion along the border—the woman in "A Servant to Servants" for example, whose mind is as hemmed in as the lake she gazes out upon; or the old man of "An Old Man's Winter Night," trapped in a house where "all out of doors looked darkly in at him"; or the witch of Coos, who, living with her mentally arrested son, finds her imaginative release in rehearsing for a stranger her half-forged, half-pathetic ghost story. Above all, there is the poet himself, who feels the terror of loneliness. Caught alone in the woods beneath the onset of winter's first snow, he feels the full threat of alien forces, and, although he knows that "all the precedent" is on his side and that spring *will* come again, he stumbles,

> looking up and round,
> As one who overtaken by the end
> Gives up his errand, and lets death descend
> Upon him where he is, with nothing done
> To evil, no important triumph won,
> More than if life had never been begun.

In these moments of terror, the outer threat of nature, with its ominous woods, its appalling snow, its rustling leaves hissing along the ground, gives rise to the deepest inner fears. The entire landscape becomes a haunting reflection of psychic desolation. If Frost can contemplate the infinity of space with a certain equanimity it is not because he feels more secure than Pascal but because, as he says,

> I have it in me so much nearer home
> To scare myself with my own desert places.

Confronting these desert places of his landscape, Frost needs all the restraint at his command, for the dark woods possess a magnetic attraction drawing him spellbound into them. The trees, whose branches reach out toward him and whose leaves insistently whisper an invitation, are, as Frost has written, the "vague dream heads" come out of the ground to beckon him to succumb to the mystery of their depths. Frost finds his power of resistance and control in the measured language of poetry—he even speaks of the poem as a "momentary stay against confusion." And he loves the metered line, choosing to leave free verse to Carl Sandburg on the ground that he, Frost, "would as soon write free verse as play tennis with the net down."

The haunting rhythms of "Stopping by Woods on a Snowy Evening" express the powerful fascination the woods have upon the lonely traveler, who, in the face of a long journey, descending night, and falling snow, pauses in the gathering gloom of the "darkest evening of the year," transfixed by the compelling invitation of the forest:

> Whose woods these are I think I know.
> His house is in the village though;
> He will not see me stopping here
> To watch his woods fill up with snow.
>
> My little horse must think it queer
> To stop without a farmhouse near
> Between the woods and frozen lake
> The darkest evening of the year.
>
> He gives his harness bells a shake
> To ask if there is some mistake.
> The only other sound's the sweep
> Of easy wind and downy flake.
>
> The woods are lovely, dark and deep,
> But I have promises to keep,
> And miles to go before I sleep,
> And miles to go before I sleep.

The poem is *about* the spell of the woods—the traveler's own woods, we want to say, but they are alien enough and belong to someone else enough for him to sense the trespass of his intent gaze into them at the same time he recognizes their sway over him. His heightened awareness projects his concern for himself back to the representatives of civilization, the unseen owner of the woods and the horse in harness. Thus, the indifferent animal becomes, in his master's alerted imagination, the guardian who sounds the alarm which rings above the whispered invitation.

The poem *is* the counter-spell against the invitation, the act by which the traveler regains dominion of his will. The intricately interlocked rhyme scheme (*aaba, bbcb, ccdc, dddd*) and the strict iambic tetrameter, while they imitate and suggest the hypnotic power of the forest, also form the basis of a protective charm against that power. The logic of the rhyme scheme, in which the divergent third line of one stanza becomes the organizing principle of the next, is an expression of the growing control and determination described in the syntax. Thus, the first line of the last quatrain finally *names* the nature of the spell and also provides the term which is answered in rhyme by the poet's decision to refuse the invitation.

Seen in this light, the poem reveals what Frost means when he says that "every poem written regular is a symbol small or great of the way the will has to pitch into the commitments deeper and deeper to a rounded conclusion. . . ." He sees the form as both instrument and embodiment of the will braving the alien entanglements of experience—the commitments—for it must organize and at the same time contain its material. The poem in its totality is the image of the will in action, and the poet's spirit and courage convert words into deeds. The words are the given, and "We make them do," he says, and continues: "Form in language is such a disjected lot of old broken pieces it seems almost non-existent as the spirit till the two embrace in the sky." In the completed poem both form and spirit have encountered not "in rivalry but in creation." The creation is not a forging of a new world, but the discovery and grasp of a world at once familiar and strange. The act of writing is, to return to the statement I have quoted earlier, a plunge into the vast chaos the poet has lived through and a bringing into the full range of consciousness as much of that half-known life as possible. That is the meaning of self-possession.

And Frost, like the Paul Bunyan in "Paul's Wife," is a terrible possessor; indeed, the action of that poem recapitulates Frost's own process of creation. In the pith of an unsound saw log abandoned in disgust by the practical sawyer, Paul discovered the material which, after he had delicately carved it out and carefully dipped it in the waters of a mountain lake, emerged into consciousness to become the fabled wife whom he protected from the brute tribute to beauty offered by the curious lumbermen:

> Owning a wife with him meant owning her.
> She wasn't anybody else's business,
> Either to praise her, or so much as name her,
> And he'd thank people not to think of her.

> Murphy's idea was that a man like Paul
> Wouldn't be spoken to about a wife
> In any way the world knew how to speak.

Frost too has gone back into the desolation of a world abandoned to seize his own particular kind of beauty.

Of course, he has shared it with the world, but he clings fiercely to his poems as his private property, and even the titles of his several volumes describe the progress of his endeavor to lay claim to his world. From "A Boy's Will" he went on to define his province, "North of Boston," and in "Mountain Interval," "New Hampshire," and "West Running Brook," he established enough landmarks within the region to open what he calls "A Further Range." In "A Witness Tree," the tree, once a part of the wilder woods, bears the wound he has given it as a witness of his ownership, and Frost himself assumes the rôle of landowner, leading his reader along the boundaries of his property. Finally, in "Steeple Bush," the hardhack flowering at the edge of the clearing stands as the precious item he holds against the ever-returning woods. The property he reclaims from the ruins of time he insistently refuses to relinquish:

> I could give all to Time except—except
> What I myself have held. But why declare
> The things forbidden that while the Customs slept
> I have crossed to safety with? For I am there
> And what I would not part with I have kept.

Frost's long career of returning into his own to enlarge his province has been a continual thrust of both will and memory, and he quite logically defines the initial delight of making a poem as the "surprise of remembering something I didn't know I knew." If there are times when his poetry fails, as in the editorializing poems which have been increasing in ratio until they fairly dot "Steeple Bush," he fails because he is remembering something he knew all the time, and his poetry hardens into provincial cynicism. Although critics have lamented this departure from the earlier lyric and dramatic vein, Frost's penchant for bald statement followed as necessarily from his earlier poem as self-assurance follows self-possession. Moreover, out of this almost brash assurance comes "Directive," surely one of Frost's highest achievements.

Here the poet is not the listener or the narrator, but the confident guide leading his reader back into a "time made simple by the loss/ of detail," to discover among the ruins of a vacant farm the broken goblet the guide has hidden under a cedar tree against the day of his return. The broken goblet, originally cast aside by the adults as a mere toy for the children's playhouse and again abandoned when everyone departed, becomes the all important detail which the poet has seized to save from the ruins of the past. It is for Frost an image of the charmed grail itself, a talisman not carried like a spear of grass but stored away in a secret niche and displayed only to the right persons who, following the poet along the intricate pathways toward the heart of his property, are lost enough to find themselves. Possessing this charm, they can, by drinking with him from the waters of the brook which once supplied water for the farmhouse, "be whole again beyond confusion."

Yet Frost maintains a sharp comic detachment from the central association he exploits, the allusion to the grail quest. His poem is not a recapitulation or variation of the legend but a masque, a performance staged for his audience's benefit by the knowing god who owns the salvaged grail. His whimsy—he "only has at heart our getting lost" and he has hidden the goblet "so the wrong ones can't find it"—is actually an aspect of his comic delicacy as he leads his followers through the "serial ordeal" of being watched from "forty cellar holes," and on to the "height of the adventure" which is the height of ground where two village cultures "faded into each other." The chapel perilous is the field "no bigger than a harness gall" marked by a collapsing cellar hole where once a farmhouse stood, and the grail turns out to be the broken goblet stolen from the children's playhouse.

These are the discrepancies which Frost almost mockingly exploits as he conducts the journey, but they are also the miraculous details which authoritatively affirm the reality of this search as opposed to the legendary quest. The guide's command comes from knowing every detail of his private ground, details which were hard to come by but which are securely his own. Even the resurgent woods receive a brashly tender notice as they pass beneath the guide's vision:

> As for the woods' excitement over you
> That sends light rustle rushes to their leaves,
> Charge that to upstart inexperience.

> Where were they all not twenty years ago?
> They think too much of having shaded out
> A few old pecker-fretted apple trees.

In his way an audacious brag, the guide yet makes good on all his claims—and well he might, for "Directive" rehearses the course Frost has pursued as a poet and is thus a survey of the ground he has possessed. But it also points toward what is to come, toward the masques and beyond to his latest poem, "Kitty Hawk," in which, while commemorating the Wright brothers' famous flight, he seizes the chance to celebrate his own first flight into poetry with his sacred muse—an event which considerably anticipated the first propeller-driven flight.

Finally, "Directive" is a performance by the same "character" who so often commands the central stage as lecturer and whose public performances imitate to a remarkable degree the structure of his poems. For Frost's primal subject is always poetry and the poet—*his* poetry and himself the poet. Beginning in conversational manner, he utters a summary remark about the state of the world, the nature of woman, or the status of science. This aptly stated phrase constitutes the ostensible subject for the evening, and, although he returns to it periodically, his digressions move in ever widening arcs until the initial theme reveals itself as but an association leading toward what is Frost's most private and most public possession—his poems. Even in this introductory movement, Frost is already retreating from his audience toward himself, and the conversational idiom functions as an invitation, never as an appeal.

When he reaches the poems he is to "say," as he puts it, Frost has gained a presence of remote loneliness. His manner of "saying" them is neither recitative, declamatory, nor bardic; rather he seems to be remembering each poem as he moves through it, and even when he forgets his way he usually chooses to find himself without benefit of text. There is a manifest anticipation both in speaker and audience as the remembering proceeds, a kind of wonder and suspense as the tenuous thread of the poem is pursued; and when the end is grasped there is a distinct sense of discovery *and* relief. The disparaging remarks which may be, and have been, leveled at Frost's mode of delivery—at his flatness of voice, his frequent pauses, and his halting delivery—are dwarfed by the essential victory achieved on every poem. And much of his success as a reader of his poems stems from his ability to convey this sense of achievement and repossession.

To know Frost's poems and then to watch his mind close tenderly about them is to see again that they are his triumphs in form wrought out of the chaos he has lived through. They are for him the living emblems—the charms which must be *said*—that, like the broken goblet, he has reclaimed from his abandoned experience and ours. Thus, when Frost, speaking for himself and his muse in "Kitty Hawk," says

> This we're certain of,
> All we do and try
> All we really love
> Is to signify . . .

he is celebrating in poetic language the labor of a lifetime.

Isadore Traschen

Robert Frost: Some Divisions in a Whole Man

Robert Frost wrote some of the finest verse of our time. He created his own extraordinarily flat, "unpoetic" variant of the conversational idiom which has become the medium of most modern poetry. He restricted himself to the homeliest diction, to words largely of one or two syllables, a remarkable feat. And he countered this simplicity with a highly sophisticated rhetoric, with the devious twistings of the poem's development, with the irony of simple word and subtle thought. His diction was just right for the rural scene he chose in the face of the intimidating international subjects of Eliot and Pound, and just right, too, for its simple particulars. He was no doubt our master of the realistic particular. Things magnified at his touch; they seemed to live. His themes were familiar to most, and appealed—though in widely varying degrees—to everyone: the exhaustion of living, the sense of imminent danger (large as the ocean, small as a spider), personal isolation, the need for community. Frost is so good, so much pleasure to read that you wonder why he needs to be defended so often.

From *The Yale Review*, LV (October, 1965), 57-70. Published with the permission of *The Yale Review*, copyright Yale University.

36

What is it about him that makes even enthusiastic admirers like Randall Jarrell—whose appreciation, "To the Laodiceans," should be read by everyone—begin by acknowledging his limitations? After all, everyone has them. Is there some really critical defect in him, one that might explain why Frost never had the passionate following Eliot had? Why didn't Frost so affect us, so transform us that we had no choice but to be his?

What I want to do is develop an aspect of Frost's poems which I feel represents such a defect. I am aware of the exceptions to what I have to say: these will be occasionally noted. My principal argument is that Frost never risked his life, his whole being; he was never really lost, like the Eliot of *The Waste Land*. He remained in control, in possession of himself. He did this by keeping himself from the *deepest* experiences, the kind you stake your life on. And this is reflected in various ways, all of which point to a central division in Frost's experience, in himself. He has been represented, by himself as well as by others, as one able to integrate his life. "Drink and be whole again beyond confusion," he advised in "Directive," written during the Second World War; and confused as we were, we were grateful for the recipe. Again, in "Education by Poetry," he says the "Greatest of all attempts to say one thing in terms of another is the philosophical attempt to say matter in terms of spirit, or spirit in terms of matter, to make the final unity . . . it is the height of all poetry, the height of all thinking." But when we read his poetry we encounter division, of several kinds.

To begin with, it has been pointed out that though Frost looks at nature closely, and renders it faithfully, he often fails to fuse his idea of it with his feeling. Thus poems like "Tuft of Flowers," "Two Tramps in Mud Time," and "Hyla Brook" divide in two: the things described, the pure existent, free of any abstraction, and the abstract comment, the moral or philosophical lesson in the tradition of Longfellow and Emerson, whom he admired. Take "Hyla Brook," less known than the others:

> By June our brook's run out of song and speed.
> Sought for much after that, it will be found
> Either to have gone groping underground
> (And taken with it all the Hyla breed
> That shouted in the midst a month ago,
> Like ghost of sleigh-bells in a ghost of snow) —
> Or flourished and come up in jewelweed,

Weak foliage that is blown upon and bent,
Even against the way its waters went.
Its bed is left a faded paper sheet
Of dead leaves stuck together by the heat—
A brook to none but who remember long.
This as it will be seen is other far
Than with brooks taken otherwhere in song.
We love the things we love for what they are.

The poem is a marvel of simple particulars enhanced by homely metaphors and the distinctively Frost idiom, concluding with the abstract comment. In this case the comment is at odds with the spirit of the poem: if we love the things we love for what they are we had better resist setting up a philosophy about them. Often, in this way, Frost does not resolve his identification with particulars and his separation from them by laying on a general meaning. His poetry reveals a division between the imagist and the commentator, between the man who sees and the man who abstracts, between the naturalist and the rationalist. In some remarks on Edwin Arlington Robinson, Frost says, "I am not the Platonist Robinson was. By Platonist I mean one who believes what we have here is an imperfect copy of what is in heaven." But the structure of many of his poems, an ascent from matter to idea, is Platonic. I do not mean to imply that Frost thought matter inferior to the idea; he is frequently skeptical about the mind's way of knowing, as in "Bond and Free," where love is superior to thought by virtue of its existential involvement: by "simply staying [it] possesses all." Still, it is fair to say that the structure of his poems often gives the impression that matter, or, more generally, existence is an illustration of an idea.

The dramatic narratives ("The Death of the Hired Man," "A Servant of Servants," etc.) are exceptions to Frost's Platonic structure. Because of the form, probably, the action is sustained all the way; no formulation is tagged on; these poems are memorable in themselves, free of abstract wisdom. Of course this fusion of image and idea happens on occasion in the lyrics, as in "The Silken Tent" and "The Most of It," and with fine effect. Here is the less known "Silken Tent," in which the theme of love and bondage of "Bond and Free" is fused in a one-sentence sonnet with the metaphysical skill of Donne or Marvell.

She is as in a field a silken tent
At midday when a sunny summer breeze

> Has dried the dew and all its ropes relent,
> So that in guys it gently sways at ease,
> And its supporting central cedar pole,
> That is its pinnacle to heavenward
> And signifies the sureness of the soul,
> Seems to owe naught to any single cord,
> But strictly held by none, is loosely bound
> By countless silken ties of love and thought
> To everything on earth the compass round,
> And only by one's going slightly taut
> In the capriciousness of summer air
> Is of the slightest bondage made aware.

But this fusion is not characteristic. Generally, there is a division between subject matter and idea, and the poem suffers. The abstract ending contracts the poem; it freezes and flattens the feelings set in motion, channeling them into an idea, as though the idea were the really important part of the poem, its telos.

This division in Frost is reflected in the frequent disjunction between his subject matter and his verse rhythms. The meter is varied from poem to poem; the iambic measure has a human voice, a quiet one which secures a tension between the dramatic substance and its own effortlessness. Yet as we read a number of poems at a stretch, another effect emerges, one of monotony—especially, as Yvor Winters points out, in those in blank verse. It is as though Frost brings an *a priori* rhythm to each poem, a further Platonic tendency: the *idea* of a rhythm distinct from the matter it will give form to. You get the same rhythm in a poem of rural manners like "Mending Wall," with its theme of community, as you do in a quasi-tragic piece like "An Old Man's Winter Night," with its theme of isolation. The poems call for different intensities of feeling, but there is little evidence of this in the rhythms. Compare Frost's verse with that of Shakespeare and Donne:

> The expense of spirit in a waste of shame
> Is lust in action.

> Batter my heart, three-person'd God; for, you
> As yet but knocke, breathe, shine, and seeke to mend.

Among other things, what makes the earlier poets unmonotonous in their rhythms is the weight of the stressed syllables; this further breaks the even flow. Frost rarely breaks up, rarely staggers under the burden of his subject; his tone is level even when the theme is disintegration. The tone is right in poems of meditation like "After Apple-Picking" and "Stopping By Woods on a Snowy Evening"; here there is a happy fusion of tone, rhythm and matter. The effect of his tone and rhythms is generally one of understatement—all to the good in the modern canon. But continual understatement acts as an anodyne, beguiling us into what we like to believe is the quiet voice of wisdom. This may have been all right in more contemplative times; but I would think our age is more authentically expressed through pain, through the pure, simple scream it would have been so *pleasant* to hear at times in Frost's poems. Frost's "monotony" may be connected with his philosophic attitude, an even-tempered sceptical rationalism which has been a dominant tradition in Western culture since Plato and Aristotle. It has little in common with another tradition, that of the great howlers who risked everything: the Old Testament prophets, Job (the triviality of "A Masque of Reason" is revealing in this connection), the Greek tragic playwrights and Shakespeare, or romantics like Blake and Rimbaud.

Frost's incapacity for the tragic howl is of a piece, I believe, with the sentimentality which marks a further division in him, the separation of fact and feeling. A typical instance is "The Road Not Taken," with its elegiac air:

> I shall be telling this with a sigh
> Somewhere ages and ages hence:
> Two roads diverged in a wood, and I—
> I took the one less traveled by,
> And that has made all the difference.

Frost acknowledges that life has limits ("knowing how way leads on to way"), yet he indulges himself in the sentimental notion that we could be really different from what we have become. He treats this romantic cliché on the level of the cliché; hence the appeal of the poem for many. But after having grown up, who still wants to be that glamorous movie star or ball player of our adolescent daydreams? In "The Jolly Corner" James saw the other road leading to corruption, the fate of those who deny themselves, who suffer a division of the self.

These divisions in Frost may help us see what is unsatisfactory about a finely wrought poem like "The Onset."

> Always the same, when on a fated night
> At last the gathered snow lets down as white

As may be in dark woods, and with a song
It shall not make again all winter long
Of hissing on the yet uncovered ground,
I almost stumble looking up and round,
As one who overtaken by the end
Gives up his errand, and lets death descend
Upon him where he is, with nothing done
To evil, no important triumph won,
More than if life had never been begun.

Yet all the precedent is on my side:
I know that winter death has never tried
The earth but it has failed: the snow may heap
In long storms an undrifted four feet deep
As measured against maple, birch, and oak,
It cannot check the peeper's silver croak;
And I shall see the snow all go down hill
In water of a slender April rill
That flashes tail through last year's withered brake
And dead weeds, like a disappearing snake.
Nothing will be left white but here a birch,
And there a clump of houses with a church.

Frost is again divided in his response. He resists winter and welcomes spring; he welcomes life but does not see that death is organic to it. Later, in "West-running Brook," he was to say that "The universal cataract of death" sends up our life. But Frost largely flirted with the dark woods that appear with some frequency in his poems; he was not lost in them deeply enough as Dante was to be transformed. Instead, he made a "strategic retreat."

If Frost's resistance to death is unnatural, his sense of spring in "The Onset" is incomplete. It lacks the organic singleness of spring and winter of Dylan Thomas' "The force that through the green fuse drives the flower / Drives my green age; that blasts the roots of trees / Is my destroyer." What is also lacking is the pain of birth, as in Lawrence's "Tortoise Shout." Here is the tortoise

. . . in the spasm of coition, tupping like a jerking leap, and oh!
Opening its clenched face from his outstretched neck
And giving that fragile yell, that scream,
Super-audible,
From his pink, cleft, old-man's mouth,

> Giving up the ghost,
> Or screaming in Pentecost, receiving the ghost.

Some of this is prosy, but it has a power which if Frost had exercised might have shaken many of his admirers. For Frost spring is simply another occasion for his even-tempered reassurance, compounded in the idyllic image of houses and church worthy of Norman Rockwell. Quietly brought in, sparely set down, pretty to contemplate . . . yet effective only if we allow ourselves to be coerced by the idyl of the American village. But after Winesburg and Spoon River and Lardner? The village church is pretty to look at, but too often filled with people divided in their own ways: loving mankind but fearing if not hating Catholics, Jews, and Negroes, not to speak of foreigners. As a matter of fact, in "A Star in a Stone-Boat," in the same *New Hampshire* volume, Frost is ironic about those who "know what they seek in school and church."

Now "The Onset" hints at difficulties, but these are overlooked or forgotten in the interests of the pleasant solution. The speaker says he is like one who "lets death descend / Upon him where he is, with nothing done / To evil, no important triumph won, / More than if life had never been begun." This is a characterization of the Laodicean temper comparable to Yeats' "The best lack all conviction," or Eliot's "We who were living are now dying / With a little patience." But Frost does not draw the conclusions Yeats and Eliot do, or Marlow in *Heart of Darkness*, or Baudelaire, Dante, and St. John. April's slender rill will still return as life-giving as ever, untouched by Laodicean lifelessness; April will not be the cruelest month, bringing a rebirth we do not want and cannot stand. Frost's response to spring is simply no longer possible, even before the fallout, except to one who has seriously isolated himself from our times, a division I will say more about.

We have no right to demand anything of a poet but what he gives us, although we do have an obligation to define what he is giving us. Frost himself invites us to judge him, in the terms I have set forth, in one of his great poems, "The Gift Outright." He says that before we were the land's

> Something we were withholding made us weak
> Until we found out that it was ourselves
> We were withholding from the land of living . . .

You must give yourself, surrender yourself, fully to realize your-self. Curiously, this is the point of the first poem, "Into My Own," in Frost's first volume; by going into the woods he will be "more sure of all I thought was true." But Frost generally separates him-self from nature, as when he speaks with an oddly exploitative élan of our increasing "hold on the planet"; unlike Wordsworth, who identifies with nature as his spirit is "Rolled round in earth's diurnal course, / With rocks, and stones, and trees." Now there is a sense of fully meeting nature in "After Apple-Picking," but usually, as in "Come In" or "Stopping by Woods," the poet only seems to give himself, while actually withdrawing. Robert Penn Warren explains the withdrawal in "Stopping by Woods" as "man defining himself by resisting the pull of nature." No doubt we must *distinguish* ourselves from the rest of nature, but we cut ourselves off from a critical part of our existence if we do this by *resisting*. This may lead, for example, to the kind of alienation Lawrence dramatizes in "Snake." A venomous, golden snake appears and "The voice of my education said to me / He must be killed." He throws a log at it, forcing the kingly animal to retreat, "convulsed in undignified haste." He has despoiled nature, and it weighs on him like an albatross: "I missed my chance with one of the lords / of life. / And I have something to expiate; / A pettiness." Some-times, as in the beautiful "Oven Bird," Frost seems to identify with nature, but even here he is really personifying the bird, im-posing his philosophical mood of the moment: "The question that he [the bird] frames in all but words / Is what to make of a diminished thing."

The difference between Frost and Lawrence and Thomas is critical. Lawrence defines his humanness in a mutual encounter with nature, Frost by resisting it. The tortoise's pain is Lawrence's, as Thomas is bent by the same wintry fever as the crooked rose. Both become more profoundly human by surrendering, or at least immersing themselves in nature. They *grow* out of their relation to it; Frost does not because he is curiously divided from it, observing it to introduce his own ideas. He does not sink to come up new; he cannot lose himself, follow his own advice and surrender himself; he will not let go of himself, allow nature to work on him and change him. As a sceptic, the poet of the middle way, not committing himself to extremes—passional or intellectual—Frost remains separate from the objects he looks at, unchanged. There is no mutual penetration which transforms subject and object. Two impulses work against each other, the naturalistic and the civilized, and the latter prevails. Despite all the suggestions of disaster in his poetry Frost does not really disturb us. He is all too frequently prepared to reach some reasonable agreement. Problems—yes; but solutions too.

What all this comes to is a detachment which in its cultural context is a poetry of isolationism. This is obviously appealing to an American audience. The title of his first volume, *A Boy's Will*, alludes to the favorite American poet of the nineteenth century, Longfellow, and to the poem which appeals to our nostalgia as well as our Edenic impulse. Succeeding titles—*North of Boston, Mountain Interval, New Hampshire, West-running Brook*—all reassure us of the importance, the validity, the worth not merely of our country, but of that part where we began and where our virtues were seeded and flourished. Nor do the images which trouble that scene—the hired man, the servant of servants, and the others—trouble Frost's audience; on the contrary, the harsh realism validates its nostalgia. Rural America is offered as the theatre of this world, appealing to anyone who would like to forget the world.

Delmore Schwartz once called T. S. Eliot our international hero; Frost is our national, isolationist hero, withdrawn as Americans generally are from the dialogue of ideas which give form to living not only in our time but at least as far back as the Old Testament days. Typical of Frost's attitude are the words of the wife in "In the Home Stretch": "New is a word for fools in towns who think / Style upon style in dress and thought at last / Must get somewhere." Nothing could be more appealing to our traditionalist temper; nothing is more alien to our revolutionary tradition; nothing could be plain sillier. The wife is not aware that whatever ideas *she* has are the new ones of Moses, the Prophets, the Greek philosophers, Christ, St. Paul, St. Thomas, Montaigne, Newton, Marx, and Freud. To ignore the ideas of *our* age means that you use them uncritically, for they get into your bones anyway.

Intellectual heat has tempered most of us; but Frost "is able," as Robert Langbaum says, "to shrug off those conflicts between man and nature, thought and reality, head and heart, science and religion, which since the romantic period have torn other poets apart." As a consequence, many of his poems which seem to bear upon our crises do not really confront them. For example, "Once By the Pacific" warns of "a night of dark intent / . . . and not only a night, an age." But it lacks the specific historical sense of Yeats's "Leda and the Swan," "Two Songs from a Play," and "The Second Coming," and so has only a vague effect. Yeats inter-

prets the historical moments and so involves himself in them
as he gives us a way of understanding them. Uninvolved, Frost
paralyzes us with merely passive or stunned responses to terror,
as in "Design," "Bereft," or "Once By the Pacific"; he does not
take up the arms of the intellect against our sea of troubles. Failing to be involved, he falls back on eternal commonplaces. In "The
Peaceful Shepherd" he points out that the cross, the crown, and
the scales of trade all might as well have been the sword; in
"November" he deplores "The waste of nations warring"; in "A
Question" he asks if life is worth all the suffering. These poems do
not pretend to much, but their very simplicity allows us to see
more readily the commonplace quality of so much of Frost's
thought, owing, I would say, to his separation from the intellectual
wars of our time.

Frost's withdrawal from the exhausting scene of the mind, of a
piece with his withdrawal from the pain in nature, his moralizing
use of nature, and his dreamlike response to it—all this can lead
to the cruelty of neglect. (Though being *in* the wars of the mind
hardly exempts one from cruelty as such.) The highly praised
"The Lesson for Today" is very witty, often brilliant, and absolutely heartless in its trite equation of our epoch with other dark
ones, particularly so when we remember it was written in 1941.
Swinging on one's philosophic swivel, it may be valid to say "One
age is like another for the soul," or that "all ages shine / with
equal darkness." But this is much like Gertrude, who used the
vulgar argument that death is common to all, and therefore why
so particular with Hamlet. Hamlet is a tragic figure because what
happened *was* particular to him, just as what has happened *is*
particular to us—how else can we take it seriously? It is the particulars that speak to us, that it would be obscene to ignore or
forget. The poet who maintains his balance before the ideas and
events which are unbalancing the rest of us risks being irrelevant.
To equate one age with another is to be outside of both. How
different Frost seems when he does render modern particulars, as
at the end of "The Bonfire"—not one of his better poems, certainly. Speaking to some children, he asks,

> Haven't you heard, though,
> About the ships where war has found them out
> At sea, about the towns where war has come
> Through opening clouds at night with droning speed
> Further o'erhead than all but stars and angels—

And children in the ships and in the towns?
Haven't you heard what we have lived to learn?
Nothing so new—something we had forgotten:
War is for everyone, for children too.
I wasn't going to tell you and I mustn't.
The best way is to come up hill with me
And have our fire and laugh and be afraid.

But once again it is "Nothing so new. . . ."

When Frost confronts our civilization in its totality—the encounter that defines our great moderns, as Stephen Spender has pointed out—he is inadequate; all he can muster is a commonplace. Perhaps he is prone to aphorisms in a poem dealing with the modern scene because he does not see it. He talks about it, but is incapable of creating its personae, like Eliot's carbuncular clerk. Having committed himself to by-road, rural figures not shaped by central modern concerns, he falls into archness or waspishness when dealing with features of our world—and not least, incidentally, its representative literature. In the later, rightly admired "Directive," he advises us to retreat from "all this now too much for us" back to a "time made simple by the loss / of detail." Here once more is the refusal to confront the particulars of our world; after a journey which Frost invites us to compare with that of a Grail knight, yet with only a hint of the Grail trials, we will be saved, "be whole again beyond confusion" by drinking the cup of the past, the simple time. Comforting . . . but after Eliot's fragmented Fisher King? Langbaum comments that Frost's poetry is the kind "that delivers us from the poignancy of the historical moment to place us in contact with a survival-making eternal folk wisdom. We can live by Frost's poetry as we could not by Yeats's or Pound's." On the contrary. The poetry that disturbs us most strengthens us most, much the way the tragic hero affirms himself by acknowledging the last truth. Eternal wisdom is comic to those conscious of the awful fact of *this* historic moment. Divided from our time, Frost, our wisdom-poet, has so little of the kind of wisdom appropriate to our time, the hellish, existential wisdom of Kafka and Camus, or the biological wisdom of Lawrence.

In his famous speech celebrating Frost's eighty-fifth birthday Lionel Trilling links Frost with the tragic poets. He makes this assertion with an unusual rhetorical violence: "when ever have people been so isolated, so lightning-blasted, so tried down and calcined by life, so reduced, each in his own way, to some last irreducible core of being." Professor Trilling protests too much. He ignores most of Frost's poetry, with its scepticism, rationalism, strategic retreats, and low key—all of which make for a small voice. The tragic sense is best realized in characters highly developed in mind and spirit, not present in Frost. And it requires something else, a particular, coherent vision of life—for example, Christian, as with Eliot; aristocratic, as with Yeats; Apollonian, as with Mann. This vision shapes the tragic hero and makes him a worthy antagonist of the forces of ruin—so in "The Waste Land," "Nineteen Hundred and Nineteen," and *Death in Venice*. Without this coherent vision you have only one half of the tragic drama—only ruin, which by itself is sentimental. Perhaps it was owing to his scepticism and his generally pragmatic outlook that Frost did not develop this vision.

The great moderns have thought steadily about our age; from this has come intense commitments taking the form of those consistent visions of modern life which have shaped our imagination. What distinguishes them, as Spender has put it, is their sense of the present "as a fatal knowledge that has overtaken the whole of civilization and has broken the line of tradition with the past." Frost writes in a historical vacuum, with almost nothing to say to us about the modern content of our alienation and fragmentation. His efforts here yield little that has not been more passionately and tragically said by many others. "Departmental" is a fairly good, if too clever poem on specialization; but "Why Wait for Science" and "Bursting Rapture" are pebbly rather than Vermont granite; the latter even childish when we think of Yeats' treatment of the apocalyptic theme in "The Second Coming" and his other annunciation poems. No one seems to be more solidly planted in the world, yet no one of Frost's stature tells us less about our world.

It is the absence of a modern texture which in one way gives Frost his special appeal to moderns. As a poet of particulars, especially of nature, Frost has an effect on the city person s   e-thing like that Wordsworth had for John Stuart Mill. For such a person—especially a bookish one—Frost brings a momentary salvation. He restores the *things* that our organized way of living and our abstract way of seeing have obliterated: "Blueberries as big as the end of your thumb," or an ax-helve "slender as a whipstock, / Free from the least knot, equal to the strain / Of bending like a sword across the knee." And in making us see these things he saturates us with the texture of American life, the life of its beginnings. This too is good for the intellectual who for many reasons (the cant, hypocrisy, and immorality of public life, the spiritual deterioration of private life) often feels like an outsider in his own country. Frost has reminded us of all that cannot be spoiled by the politician or the brassy patriot. For this we are grateful. Blueberries, ax-helves, birches, oven birds—these are stable vantage points, solid stations—but not enough. They are the moving particulars common to any time, not the disturbing particulars of our own. Neither his images nor his scenes are modern; his isolation provides him only with situations out of another era. Our representative heroes are fated in images drawn from the modern world: Joseph K. crucified by the celestial bureaucracy, Meursault by the apparatus of the law, reflecting conventional, middle-class values. Irving Howe says that "Frost writes as a modern poet who shares in the loss of firm assumptions." Perhaps, but this could apply equally to Donne or Montaigne. Yvor Winters' remarks on Frost as a thinker are more pertinent. "Frost's scepticism and uncertainty do not appear to have been so much the result of thought as the result of the impact upon his sensibility of conflicting notions of his own era—they appear to be the result of his having taken the easy way and having drifted with the various currents of his time." Frost is contemporary rather than modern. He lives in our time but at bottom is not affected, disturbed, shaken, transformed by it. Everyone rightly praises "An Old Man's Winter Night," but "Gerontion," drawing on fewer particulars of old age, disturbs us more, for it is a portrait of old age in our age, and so becomes a portrait of our age.

The division in much of Frost's poetry between image and idea, matter and rhythm, the naturalist and the rationalist is reflected in Frost's withholding himself from nature, and this in turn we see is a reflection of the division between his subject matter and that of the age. This was fatal to his full development, preventing the kind of growth and transformations that marked Yeats and Eliot. His simplicity and homeliness probably contributed to this fate. He took these qualities too seriously, as though they were the heart of truth. He became his own imitator, beguiling himself enough to keep out of the complexities and contentions of our time, out of the political, moral, religious, and philosophical crises which might have led to a passionate commitment. Even if wrong-headed, this at least would have opened hell to him.

2. Figures of Poems

Alvan S. Ryan

Frost and Emerson: Voice and Vision

I

Are Frost and Emerson poets in the same tradition? There are superficial similarities. They agree on the central importance of symbol and metaphor. They have a common preoccupation with rural subjects. They share a basic sense of "correspondences," though the differences here are also important. Their experiments with various meters and verse forms, their use of dialogue, their fondness for epigrammatic statement—both have written a great deal of gnomic verse—are also evident. The very titles of some of Frost's poems ("Mending Wall," "Storm-Fear," "The White-Tailed Hornet," "I Could Give All to Time," "Spring Pools") carry the mind back to Emerson's "The Snow-Storm," "Give All to Love," "Two Rivers," "The Humble-Bee," "The Rhodora." But all this may indicate no more than that they turn to similar subject matter. The question still remains—and must be answered, how-

From *The Massachusetts Review,* I (October, 1959), 5-23. Reprinted by permission of *The Massachusetts Review,* © 1959 The Massachusetts Review, Inc.

ever briefly: What of their poetic theories and practice of poetry?

For Emerson the poet's role is essentially bardic and prophetic; invariably the definitions have religious overtones. Before he is maker, the poet is prophet, priest and seer. Through his imagination and intuitive powers he penetrates the hidden mystery of things, apprehends their transcendent or inner reality and announces his findings to men. All this is characteristic of the nineteenth century view of the poet's role. According to Emerson the poet "has no definitions, but . . . is commanded in nature, by the living power which he feels to be there present. . . . It is nature the symbol, nature certifying the supernatural . . . which he worships. . . ." These lines from Emerson's essay "The Poet" are echoed in "Nature," the essay in which the whole section on language reveals his sense of the poet's role:

> It is not words only that are emblematic; it is things which are emblematic. Every natural fact is a symbol of some spiritual fact. . . . Who looks upon a river in a meditative hour and is not reminded of the flux of all things?

This is one side of Emerson's theory, the quintessentially transcendental or romantic note. Granting the need for further distinctions, it links him with Wordsworth, Shelley, Arnold and Whitman, and with others, such as Carlyle, who also claim for the poet the role of prophet, priest or seer.

There is nothing about Frost's conception of the role of the poet that is close to Emerson's. Frost has made few statements in prose on the poet's role, and when in his poetry he invokes the bardic attitude, as in "To a Thinker," it is with wry humor: "But trust my instinct, I'm a bard." He prefers to talk about the making of poems. As Lawrence Thompson remarks, "He has frequently suggested that he is particularly wary of hydraheaded Platonic idealism and of all those glorious risks taken by any who boldly arrive at transcendental definitions." Frost's comment on E. A. Robinson's Platonism is too well known to need quoting. But there is one passage in his "Education by Poetry" that brings Frost close to Emerson:

> Greatest of all attempts to say one thing in terms of another is the philosophical attempt to say matter in terms of spirit, or spirit in terms of matter, to make the final unity. That is the greatest

attempt that ever failed. We stop just short there. But it is the height of all poetry, the height of all thinking. . . .

Where Emerson's emphasis is on mysticism, or on some natural analogue of mystical experience closely allied to poetic intuition and inspiration, Frost is content to make a more modest and yet evocative statement:

> The figure a poem makes. . . . It begins in delight, it inclines to the impulse, it assumes direction with the first line laid down, it runs a course of lucky events, and ends in a clarification of life— not necessarily a great clarification, such as sects and cults are founded on, but in a momentary stay against confusion.

The difference in tone is not only indicative of the fuller commitment of Frost to poetry as first of all the craft of words; it also shows what has happened to the poet's sense of his role since the nineteenth century.

It is in the stress on emblem, symbol, and analogy that the theories of Emerson and Frost really meet. For Emerson the perception of analogy lies at the very root of poetry: "man is an analogist, and studies relations in all objects." The vehicle in poetry of this analogical habit is the symbol. Frost is essentially in agreement with this and he says so in his own way:

> Poetry begins in trivial metaphors, pretty metaphors, "grace metaphors," and goes on to the profoundest thinking that we have. Poetry provides the one permissible way of saying one thing and meaning another.

But he goes on to say that "All metaphor breaks down somewhere. That is the beauty of it. It is touch and go with the metaphor. . . ." Emerson, on the other hand, is less suspicious of metaphor. His whole theory is characteristically less guarded than Frost's. He speaks of the poet's "intoxication" with symbols, and sees the poet not only as using symbols, but as perceiving "the independence of the thought on the symbol, the stability of the thought, the accidency and fugacity of the symbol." In that one phrase, "the stability of the thought," there is a note that will account for one of the major differences between Emerson's poetry and Frost's.

Just as in his theory Frost sees the poet as somehow "riding" the metaphor to see where it will carry him, so, in his best poetry, the thought is too deeply implicated in the metaphor to be called independent.

But the similarities evident in the two poets are not so important as the differences, which go deep into their artistic vision. There is a far greater difference, for example, between Emerson's and Frost's poetry than between their theories. And if organic structure and symbol are central to Emerson's theory, then paradoxically Frost's poetry embodies the theory far more fully than Emerson's. Nothing makes this clearer than a comparison of the structure, the use of image and symbol, and the handling of meter and rime in much of their poetry.

Emerson's poems do not often achieve immediacy. This is so in great part because of the *a priori* nature of many of them or because of their "panoramic" quality. As a result their impact is frequently vague and general as, for example, in "The Rhodora." On the other hand, many of Frost's poems, from no matter what period, achieve an immediacy through the poet's permitting his persons not merely to speculate or muse about experience but to see and to move through the medium of literal action—action which more often than not turns finally into symbolic representation or significant generalization. "Birches," "After Apple-Picking," "Tree at My Window," "Come In," "Directive" are clear examples of this procedure.

Whereas Emerson prefers to be suggestive, to develop a few images or a series of briefly sketched scenes, Frost characteristically structures a poem around a single symbolic event. Emerson's unifying principle is ideational, Frost's metaphorical. Emerson's "The Humble-Bee," while symbolic, is also generic; Frost, in contrast, focuses on a particular "White-Tailed Hornet" whose antics demonstrate to the eye-witness the fallacy of the theory of nature's unerring aim and instinct and the danger lodged in man's worship of such illusion:

> As long on earth
> As our comparisons were stoutly upward
> With gods and angels, we were men at least, . . .
> But once comparisons were yielded downward,
> Once we began to see our images
> Reflected in the mud and even dust,
> 'Twas disillusion upon disillusion.

> We were lost piecemeal to the animals,
> Like people thrown out to delay the wolves.
> Nothing but fallibility was left us. . . .

"Woodnotes" offers a good example of Emerson's use of the panorama or catalogue, as in these lines:

> He saw the partridge drum in the woods;
> He heard the woodcock's evening hymn;
> He found the tawny thrushes' broods;
> And the shy hawk did wait for him.

This double brace of birds is the game of an eclectic hunter who scatters his shot. But Frost, whether in "Dust of Snow," "A Minor Bird," or "The Oven Bird," prefers one bird at a time.

> There is a singer everyone has heard,
> Loud, a mid-summer and a mid-wood bird,
> Who makes the solid tree trunks sound again.
> He says that leaves are old and that for flowers
> Mid-summer is to spring as one to ten.
> He says the early petal-fall is past,
> When pear and cherry bloom went down in showers
> On sunny days a moment overcast;
> And comes that other fall we name the fall.
> He says the highway dust is over all.
> The bird would cease and be as other birds
> But that he knows in singing not to sing.
> The question that he frames in all but words
> Is what to make of a diminished thing.

The habit of Frost's imagination is, in short, not like Emerson's. Rather, it is much closer to Thoreau's in its tenacious adherence to the inscapes of his world.

Stephen Whicher is right when he says that Emerson's poems "tend to slide off quickly from the fact to the idea—the cloying literariness of too much of his imagery and diction seems to represent an unsuccessful attempt to make up this deficiency of the sensuous in his verse—and they typically lack the organic, musical structure of the modern symbolist poem, since they can result only from playing off one symbol or meaning against another in a pattern of contraries." It is only in a very few of Emerson's poems

that a single metaphor or symbolic action is made into a tightly
organized and dramatic experience comparable to the best of
Frost's. "Days" is an outstanding example.

> Daughters of Time, the hypocritic Days,
> Muffled and dumb like barefoot dervishes,
> And marching single in an endless file,
> Bring diadems and fagots in their hands.
> To each they offer gifts after his will,
> Bread, kingdoms, stars, and sky that holds them all.
> I, in my pleachéd garden, watched the pomp,
> Forgot my morning wishes, hastily
> Took a few herbs and apples, and the Day
> Turned and departed silent. I, too late,
> Under her solemn fillet saw the scorn.

Here is a poem of which Frost might say that the "words comb
the idea all one way." The scene, the slow stately movement of
the verse, and the exquisitely appropriate language all work
together superbly—in a way not common in Emerson's poems.

II

The question to which I now wish to turn concerns the vision
or interpretation of experience that emerges from the total work
of each writer. This is the question that has excited the sharpest
critical debates in recent years. To compare the whole vision of
Emerson and Frost we must have a sense of the "center" of each
writer's work, yet recent criticism shows how difficult it is to find
this center. For example, any attempt to interpret Emerson's
whole vision, or to assess the major emphasis in his work, hinges
on how one sees the relation between the two Emersons—the early
Emerson of "Nature," "The Divinity School Address," "The
American Scholar" and "Self-Reliance," and the later Emerson of
such essays as "Experience" and "Illusions." The current critical
practice is to stress the Yankee realism throughout his work, or to
stress the later phase, in which there is a much profounder sense
of the complexities of human experience, a recognition of evil and
of limitation and a less ecstatic sense of the possibilities open to
the active soul. If this new reading of Emerson is valuable it should
not obscure the fact that it was the earlier Emerson of the stirring

and oracular affirmations who made so strong an impact on his contemporaries. Even if he was, as Austin Warren penetratingly suggests in his essay "Emerson, Preacher to Himself," really counseling himself in such utterances, trying to compensate for the opposite bent in his own nature, he did make them in public, and they are at the root of what we have come to think of as Emersonianism. Had the dialogue we find in his early journals been conducted in public, Emerson's impact would have been far different. The stress in the public lectures and the essays is on intuition, the moral sentiment, immediate religious experience without mediation of history, institution (church), or sacraments, and on obeying the law of one's own nature—these affirmations gave him his central place among the transcendentalists.

Nor is it quite true to say that the total interpretation of Emerson shows us a man who holds opposing truths in dialectical tension and presents his thought in the form of dialogue. If there is a dialectic, it has to be in the mind of the reader who moves through the whole body of Emerson's work and becomes aware of the differing emphases in the early and the late essays. I do not find this dialectic in the early essays and lectures. The interpretation of Emerson by Stephen Whicher is immensely illuminating; he has recovered for us a whole facet of Emerson's work that adds a new dimension to his genius. But development in a writer does not equate with a rhetorical strategy or with a philosophical view that sees in a single vision the complexities of experience and conveys this vision throughout the body of his work.

To turn to a contemporary novelist, I would say that Robert Penn Warren has precisely the type of vision that Whicher attributes to Emerson, but this to me is an unromantic and unEmersonian vision. To take another example, Carlyle's *Sartor Resartus*—which contains so many of the doctrines found in "Nature," "The Divinity School Address" and "Self-Reliance"—is not, I grant, a genuinely dialectical work. Carlyle's voluntarism and his super-charged rhetoric scarcely allow room for consideration of opposing claims. Yet in *Sartor*, Carlyle is in some ways more dialectical than Emerson. Carlyle at least creates the fiction of an English editor commenting on Teufelsdrockh's clothes philosophy, however incomplete the fiction may be.

Newton Arvin's essay "The House of Pain: Emerson and the Tragic Scene" (*Hudson Review*, Spring, 1959) and the remarks of Trilling at Frost's birthday dinner further dramatize the problem. Arvin's essay in one sense corroborates Whicher's recognition that there is far more awareness in Emerson of the problem of evil than has usually been admitted, but Arvin's final conclusion—in this sense corrective of Whicher's—is that Emerson's vision at its best is in a great religious tradition, a tradition which sees beyond tragedy to affirm the ultimate meaning even of pain and suffering. Arvin, like Pollock in his excellent essay "The Single Vision," finds unsatisfactory the view that Emerson merely reiterated the importance of intuition and spontaneity. Yet we cannot agree that Emerson can justly be reinstated for modern readers as a writer with a tragic vision. Hence Arvin affirms that in Emerson we find "the more-than-tragic emotion of thankfulness." Here, to put it briefly, we find Arvin recognizing the modern demand that a writer deal adequately with the problem of evil, but also affirming the possibility of a vision which views evil and suffering in a larger perspective.

At about the time Arvin's essay appeared, Lionel Trilling made the address that precipitated so much criticism. What did Trilling mean by calling Frost a "terrifying poet"? Clearly, in the context, he meant a tragic poet. Opening with a reference to Frost's "Sophoclean birthday," he ended by saying directly to Frost: "When I began to speak I called your birthday Sophoclean and that word has, I think, controlled everything I have said about you. Like you, Sophocles lived to a great age, writing well; and like you, Sophocles was the poet his people loved most. Surely they loved him in some part because he praised their common country. But I think that they loved him chiefly because he made plain to them the terrible things of human life: they felt, perhaps, that only a poet who could make plain the terrible things could possibly give them comfort."

It would seem difficult to give any modern poet greater praise than to compare him favorably with Sophocles, and as one reads Trilling's address and remembers his authoritative book on Matthew Arnold, two lines of Arnold's praise of Sophocles come to mind: first, the familiar line referring to him as one "who saw life steadily and saw it whole," and second, the reference to him as "Singer of sweet Colonus and its child." It is on these two notes —in Trilling's words, the praise of "their common country" and the making plain "the terrible things"—that Trilling rests his comparison of Frost and Sophocles. If Trilling's view was to be questioned, one might expect it to be questioned most strenuously by admirers of Sophocles who find Frost not of such stature. Yet, ironically, it was certain admirers of Frost who repudiated what they incomprehensibly took as Trilling's attempt to minimize Frost's significance. By their interpretation, Frost is an optimistic and benevolent singer of the emotional joy to be felt in the presence of nature, and not a "terrifying poet" at all. Moreover, one of Trilling's critics suggested that he "come out of the Freudian wood" and that he might better have invoked Emerson as one who would move familiarly in Frost's world. The comment is in line with a widely-held view that both Emerson and Frost are amiable, inspiriting, optimistic writers, who prefer to look on the pleasanter aspects of life. It is a view most effectively turned against the admirers of the two poets by a critic like Winters who holds that both Emerson and Frost turn away from the darker side of experience and abrogate their responsibility in favor of embracing a nostalgic vision of perfection.

Since it is clear that just as the more conventional estimates of the two writers bring them close together as optimists, and the severe criticism of them by Winters denigrates them for the same reason, so the more recent stress on their serious confronting of evil and limitation also brings them together, but in a very different way. To strike the balance among these three perspectives, and variations of them, is not easy. I only hope to make a start by taking a few focal points—their views of nature, of man in relation to society, of evil and suffering—for comparing Emerson's vision with Frost's.

Any understanding of Emerson's response to nature must begin with the religious attitudes central to all his thought. Rejecting the Calvinistic doctrine of total depravity and the rational theology of Unitarianism, he fastens on that same distinction between the transient and the permanent in religion made by Theodore Parker in America, Carlyle in England and numerous others in the mainstream of Transcendentalism. Like them, he fashions an eclectic synthesis of his own and turns to nature for the religious experience or sentiment. To this extent he is a transcendentalist. He rejects institutional Christianity in all its forms, while simultaneously affirming an intuitive religious experience open to all men. The most intense manifestation of this experience occurs when we attune ourselves to spiritual meanings in the contemplation of nature. This note leads, in Emerson's theory of poetry, and in much of his poetry and prose, to those sudden leaps from things, from actuality, to metaphysical affirmations. It is the flash of meaning, not the full steady confrontation of complex and ironic reality, that marks Emerson's whole attitude. And the flash of

meaning he waits for is often for him a kind of "good news" which
is no longer told in the churches. The affirmation, "God speaks,
not spaketh" of the "Divinity School Address" is a clear link
between all that he says of religion and all that he says of nature.

For Emerson the natural world mediates between man and
spiritual realities. Nature is a revelation of the eternal in the
things of sense, an avenue to the world of spirit. Granted that
many passages in his writing seem to merge God and nature in
a pantheistic way, there are numerous passages, from "Nature"
on, where he makes a clear distinction between the creative God
and His created universe. He calls the woods "the plantations of
God"; he sees a farm as a "mute gospel." It is "a sacred emblem
from the first furrow of spring to the last stack which the snow of
winter overtakes in the fields."

The early essays emphasize the beneficence of nature; they are
directed against an arid rationalistic theology that cuts man off
from the rhythms of the natural world. The intuitions of joyous
contemplation outweigh the cognizance of the darker side of nature.
Even in the essay "Nature" there is, to be sure, the section
on "Discipline" in which nature is seen as a discipline of the
understanding, but the major stress is on an emotional and intuitive response. With the essay "Experience" the more rational
response to the complexities of nature begins to dominate. Nature
"is no saint." "She comes eating and drinking and sinning." And
in "Fate," nature is "no sentimentalist. . . . The habit of snake
and spider, the snap of the tiger and other leapers and bloody
jumpers . . . these are in the system, and our habits are like
theirs." In short, there is a clear shift in emphasis between Emerson's early and later interpretation of nature, and in the search
for correspondences between man and nature which is one of his
major concerns.

Between Frost's early and late poetry there is no such shift of
emphasis from impulse or spontaneity to the recognition of evil
and limitation as is found in Emerson's essays. Frost has kept the
dialogue between feeling and thought circulating through nearly
all of his poetry, most fully in his dramatic narratives, but also in
his briefer lyrics. It is chiefly because of this that he is not Emersonian; his interpretations of experience—in his own words, his
momentary stays against confusion—are not those of either Emerson, though they are nearer to Emerson's later than to his earlier
phase.

Consider the whole theme of the correspondences between man and nature, which is so important in Emerson's prose and in his poetry. Many of Frost's poems center on this theme, and while several of them simply celebrate a brief moment of contemplation, transmuting an actual experience into a significant form, the most characteristic are those which pose a dilemma and resolve it. In one of the two or three most illuminating essays yet written on Frost's work, Robert Penn Warren traces this double attitude of acceptance and rejection in "Stopping by Woods," "Into My Own," "Come In," "After Apple-Picking" and "Birches." In each poem, as Warren shows, the speaker is strongly moved by an impulse to identify himself with nature, yet there is also the drawing back toward a properly human self-definition. In "Stopping by Woods" there is the attractiveness, the seductive and dark beauty of the woods filling up with snow. But there are also the promises to be kept. The speaker shows his humanity by his full awareness of this beauty, but he defines it finally by returning, as Warren says, "to the world of action and obligation." "We can accept neither term of the original contrast, the poem seems to say; we must find a dialectic that will accommodate both terms." Warren shows that the same conflict runs through the other poems he discusses, and that their common theme is "the idea that the reward, the dream, the ideal, stems from action and not from surrender of action."

There is a similar tension and resolution in many of Frost's other poems, especially those which recognize the mutability of nature. This mutability theme is pervasive in Romantic poetry. Romantic identification with nature oscillates between joyful celebration of nature's beauty and melancholy awareness of its transience. The ecstasy is apparent in Emerson's "Nature" and in many of his poems. The melancholy is familiar in many of the poems of Shelley, Keats and Coleridge. Frost, unlike the Romantics, defines a human attitude in the face of nature's mutability and transience either by opposition, or by seeking in nature itself a type of analogy which the Romantic poets ignore. He does not invest so heavily in nature as they do. He watches the whole curve and rhythm of the natural world and builds the human response on the minor chord in nature, and often by the very opposition Warren stresses in his essay.

The minor chord is the suggestion even in nature itself of refusal to acquiesce in mutability. "The Oven Bird" may know that "mid-

summer is to spring as one to ten," yet he continues to sing when
other birds have ceased:

> The question that he frames in all but words
> Is what to make of a diminished thing.

Again, "Hyla Brook" flows loud and swift from melting snows
and early rains, but by June has "ran out of song and speed."
Then there is left only the dry stream-bed asking, one might say,
what to make of a thing diminished to nothing.

> This as it will be seen is other far
> Than with brooks taken otherwhere in song.
> We love the things we love for what they are.

In "West-Running Brook" the central symbol is not the brook
spending itself to nothingness, but the white wave that resists the
lapsing away of the water:

> It is from that in water we were from
> Long, long before we were from any creature.

A similar theme is expressed in small compass in the sonnet,
"The Master Speed," in which the speed is, paradoxically, the
capacity for thought and meditation, the ability to stand aside
from contingency and reflect upon its meaning:

> You can climb
> Back up a stream of radiance to the sky,
> And back through history up the stream of time.
> And you were given this swiftness, not for haste
> Nor chiefly that you may go where you will,
> But in the rush of everything to waste,
> That you may have the power of standing still—
> Off any still or moving thing you say.

This same definition of a human response through opposition to
nature's mutability is also found in "A Leaf Treader." The speaker
in the poem has been treading leaves until he is "autumn-tired."
He momentarily entertains the impulse to identify his own mood
with the decay of nature, but only to reject the impulse:

> They tapped at my eyelids and touched my lips with
> an invitation to grief.
> But it was no reason I had to go because they
> had to go.
> Now, up my knee, to keep on top of another year
> of snow.

Turning from the nature themes to the dramatic poems, we find a difference in the whole approach of Emerson and Frost to the meaning of human personality—a difference that is of great significance, however difficult it may be to sum it up briefly. To deal with their conceptions of the person and society, to estimate the extent to which Frost's "individualism" is like Emerson's would require a separate essay. Certainly Frost's attitude as expressed in his poetry is closer to what is called in contemporary thought "personalism" than it is to the nineteenth century type of individualism that Emerson represents.

This difference in attitude toward personality is apparent in the very style and technique of the two writers. The essay as a form in the hands of Emerson becomes a monologue in which we overhear him conversing with himself, or a sermon in which he exhorts us to a life of virtue and of sensitivity to the ever new meaning of the universe. He can be oracular and epigrammatic, can sum up his findings on Intellect, Love, Heroism, Self-Reliance, Character, without opposition. Frost, on the other hand, has put much of his finest poetry into the form of dialogue. By so doing, he achieves the full dialectical quality that Emerson misses or, at best, achieves but partially in his essays and in his poetry. Frost is willing to sacrifice "conclusions" for dramatic immediacy and realism. He is more tentative but also more objective; the play of other personalities and the tone and cadences of other voices than his own run through all his work. The search for conclusions, for resolutions of conflicting thoughts and emotions, the impact of grief and loneliness, all are dramatized by Frost through the interplay of individual human beings.

The difference in their understanding of personality is also apparent in the contrast between Emerson's recurrent exhortation that we must transcend personality and Frost's tenacious adherence to the particularity of things as well as of people. Emerson's essay on "Love" follows Plato's "Symposium" in describing love as ultimately transcending personality and becoming love of the universal. Platonism can, to be sure, be harmonized with the Christian concept of love of God and of neighbor, but Emerson's essay does not succeed in harmonizing them. It is a cold theoretical performance, one with which even Emerson was dissatisfied. It represents a form of Platonism which Frost rejects both explicitly in prose statements and implicitly in his poetry. Love in Frost's poetry is the love of men and women for one another, for beauty, for knowledge, for things made well and with an eye to function.

It is in Frost's dramatic narratives, notably those of *North of Boston*, that his attitude toward experience is seen to be least Emersonian. There is in these poems such a full confrontation of disappointment, frustration, and failure as is not to be found in Emerson's work. In tone they have usually been called pathetic rather than tragic, yet in most of them there is a movement toward self-definition and self-knowledge that is tragic or close to the tragic. Few of Frost's protagonists are passive victims, nor do they escape into a romantic dreamworld; we see them at a moment of crisis confronting the existential situation in all its ironic reality. And they have the integrity that comes with the awareness, however dim, that more than circumstance is involved in their trials. Somehow they have chosen, and would not have it otherwise. The title of Frost's early poem, "The Trial by Existence," suggests the underlying theme of many of these poems. The fact is that the mode of these poems is closer to that of the metaphysicals than to that of the romantics. The "ideal" is entangled and interfused in the seemingly commonplace and fortuitous. For example, the action of "In the Home Stretch," from *Mountain Interval*, is simply the delivery of the furniture and belongings of a middle-aged couple from the city to the farm, where they intend to settle down for good. But the banter, the gestures, the implied criticism of their action by the furniture movers arouse second thoughts, doubts, and forebodings in the two moving to the darkness and solitude of the country. The poem lays bare the possibility of their resigning themselves to despair. The wife is tempted to; the husband keeps interposing possibilities for the future, and looks forward to inspecting "pasture, mowing, well, and brook" the next morning. The theme might be stated somewhat as follows: contentment and happiness require a certain activity of the will, a refusal to let mood drive one toward despair. The husband and wife have fashioned for themselves an image of the personal meaning of this moving to the country, but the scorn of the young city boys for country life, the oncoming darkness, the bleakness and

emptiness of the house make them suddenly question the reasons
that have led them to their choice. But when the men have left,
they regain their composure, though the husband confesses: "They
almost shook me." What is significant in such a poem is Frost's full
confronting of this sense of isolation in men, and his recognition
of the human need to master the imagination in its shifting moods.

Consideration of such poems as Frost's "A Servant to Servants,"
"The Witch of Coos," "Design," "Acquainted with the Night,"
"Once by the Pacific" would give a fuller awareness of that element
in his work which Trilling calls "terrifying." Insofar as this aspect
of Frost's work has been minimized, Trilling did a great service to
criticism in emphasizing it so effectively and so movingly. Yet these
poems and others similar in tone and theme are not the whole of
Frost. His poetry spans a wide spectrum. Celebration of form,
radiance and design in the natural order, and the lyric or dramatic
evocation of those moments when man discovers joy and reward
in his work are at one end of the spectrum. At the other end are
those poems which Trilling has in mind as being the most significant work of "his Frost." My own Frost would be closer to R. P.
Warren's than to either of these extremes. The interplay and the
tension between the human and the non-human, the sense of a
goodness in the natural order which evokes and challenges human
response without fulfilling the need for a properly human self-
definition—this is the vision, as it seems to me, that subsumes, or
perhaps connects, both extremes. And largely because it has the
dialectical and dramatic quality which Warren emphasizes, it is
an unEmersonian vision. Or to speak more accurately, if this Frost
bears some resemblance to Emerson, it is not at all to the Emerson
most critics have in mind when they compare the two. Rather,
Frost is, in the poems of the darker vision, like the Emerson
recovered by such critics as Stephen Whicher, and, in the more
serene lyrics, like Arvin's Emerson of "the more-than-tragic emotion of thankfulness." This constitutes the poetic ground on which
Frost and Emerson really meet.

Robert Penn Warren

The Themes of Robert Frost

A large body of criticism has been written on the poetry of
Robert Frost, and we know the labels which have been used:
nature poet, New England Yankee, symbolist, humanist, skeptic,
synecdochist, anti-Platonist, and many others. These labels have
their utility, true or half true as they may be. They point to something in our author. But the important thing about a poet is the
kind of poetry he writes. We are not interested primarily in his
"truth" as such—as label, as samplerwork—but in the degree to
which it is an organizing and vitalizing principle in his poem. For
only in so far as it operates as such a principle—in so far as the
poem becomes truly expressive—does the truth have meaning at
all.

In any case, I do not want to begin by quarreling with the particular labels. Instead, I want to begin with some poems and try
to see how their particular truths are operative within the poems

From *Selected Essays* by Robert Penn Warren, published by Random
House, 1958. Also appears in Roy W. Cowden, ed., *The Writer and His
Craft,* published by the University of Michigan Press, 1954. Reprinted by
permission of the William Morris Agency and the University of Michigan
Press. Copyright © 1947 by the University of Michigan Press.

themselves. I know perfectly well that there are some readers of poetry who object to this process. They say that it is a profanation, that they simply want to enjoy the poem. We all want to enjoy the poem. And we can be comforted by the fact that the poem, if it is true poem, will, like the baby's poor kitty-cat, survive all the pinching and prodding and squeezing which love will lavish upon it. It will have nine lives too. Further, and more importantly, the perfect intuitive and immediate grasp of a poem in the totality of its meaning and structure—the thing we desire—may come late rather than early—on the fiftieth reading rather than on the first. Perhaps we must be able to look forward as well as back as we move through the poem—be able to sense the complex of relationships and implications—before we can truly have that immediate grasp.

But we know that some poets flinch when faced with any critical discussion of their poems. The critic may so readily turn into the dogmatist who wants to extract the message from the poem and throw the poem away—just as the sentimentalist wants to enjoy his own feelings provoked by the poem and throw the poem away. Frost himself has been especially shy of the dogmatists and has not shown too much sympathy with a reader who, to quote him, "stands at the end of a poem ready in waiting to catch you by both hands with enthusiasm and drag you off your balance over the last punctuation mark into more than you meant to say."

Or we have the case of Yeats. An admirer sent Yeats an interpretation of one of his poems and asked if it was right. Yeats replied, grudgingly, that it was, but added that he did not think poets ought to interpret their own poems, or give the green light to the interpretations of other people, for this would serve to limit the poems.

A good poem is a massive, deep, and vital thing, but this does not imply that a poem is a stimulus to which any response, so long as it is intense, is appropriate. It does not mean that the poem is merely a body of material which the reader may fancifully reorder according to his whim. But it does imply that, though the poem is a controlled focus of experience, within the terms of that control many transliterations are possible as variants of the root attitude expressed. (There are many ways to state the theme of a poem.)

To turn to the poems: The poets may make their protests and reservations, but discussions will continue. As a starting point I am taking one of Frost's best-known and most widely anthologized pieces, "Stopping by Woods on a Snowy Evening."[1] But we shall not be content to dwell exclusively on this poem, attractive as it is, for it will quite naturally lead us into some other poems. It will lead us to the other poems because it represents but one mani-festation of an impulse very common in Frost's poetry. Here is the poem:

> Whose woods these are I think I know.
> His house is in the village though;
> He will not see me stopping here
> To watch his woods fill up with snow.
>
> My little horse must think it queer
> To stop without a farmhouse near
> Between the woods and frozen lake
> The darkest evening of the year.
>
> He gives his harness bells a shake
> To ask if there is some mistake.
> The only other sound's the sweep
> Of easy wind and downy flake.
>
> The woods are lovely, dark and deep.
> But I have promises to keep,
> And miles to go before I sleep,
> And miles to go before I sleep.

Now, the poem we are dealing with may be said to be simple—that is, the event presented is, in itself, simple and the poet says, quite simply, what the event presumably means. But this does not mean that the implications of the event are not complex; the area of experience touched upon by the poem is "suggestive" of "haunt-ing." And all good poems, even the simplest, work, it seems to me, in exactly that way. They drop a stone into the pool of our being, and the ripples spread.

The poem does, in fact, look simple. A man driving by a dark woods stops to admire the scene, to watch the snow falling into the special darkness. He remembers the name of the man who owns the woods and knows that the man, snug in his house in the vil-lage, cannot begrudge him a look. He is not trespassing. The little horse is restive and shakes the harness bells. The man decides to drive on, because, as he says, he has promises to keep—he has to get home to deliver the groceries for supper—and he has miles to go before he can afford to stop, before he can sleep.

At the literal level that is all the poem has to say. But if we read it at that level, we shall say, and quite rightly, that it is the silliest stuff we ever saw. That is what the Amazon queen in Shakespeare's *Midsummer Night's Dream* said to her husband as she watched the play Bottom and his fellows were giving in honor of her marriage. But Theseus, her husband, replied: "The best in this kind are but shadow and the worst are no worse if imagination amend them." We shall try to be a little less literal-minded than the Amazon queen and shall try to see what reality our little poem is a shadow of.

> Whose woods these are I think I know.
> His house is in the village though;
> He will not see me stopping here
> To watch his woods fill up with snow.

With that first stanza we have a simple contrast, the contrast between the man in the village, snug at his hearthside, and the man who stops by the woods. The sane, practical man has shut himself up against the weather; certainly he would not stop in the middle of the weather for no reason at all. But, being a practical man, he does not mind if some fool stops by his woods so long as the fool merely looks and does not do any practical damage, does not steal firewood or break down fences. With this stanza we seem to have a contrast between the sensitive and the insensitive man, the man who uses the world and the man who contemplates the world. And the contrast seems to be in favor of the gazer and not the owner—for the purposes of the poem at least. In fact, we may even have the question: Who is the owner, the man who is miles away or the man who can really see the woods?

With the second stanza another contrast emerges:

> My little horse must think it queer
> To stop without a farmhouse near
> Between the woods and frozen lake
> The darkest evening of the year.

Here we have the horse-man contrast. The horse is practical too. He can see no good reason for stopping, not a farmhouse near, no oats available. The horse becomes an extension, as it were, of the man in the village—both at the practical level, the level of the beast which cannot understand why a man would stop, on the darkest evening of the year, to stare into the darker darkness of the snowy woods. In other words, the act of stopping is the

specially human act, the thing that differentiates the man from
the beast. The same contrast is continued into the third stanza—
the contrast between the impatient shake of the harness bells
and the soothing whish of easy wind and downy flake.

To this point we would have a poem all right, but not much of
a poem. It would set up the essential contrast between, shall we
say, action and contemplation, but it would not be very satisfying
because it would fail to indicate much concerning the implications
of the contrast. It would be a rather too complacent poem, too
much at ease in the Zion of contemplation.

But in the poem the poet actually wrote, the fourth and last
stanza brings a very definite turn, a refusal to accept either term
of the contrast developed to this point.

> The woods are lovely, dark and deep.
> But I have promises to keep,
> And miles to go before I sleep,
> And miles to go before I sleep.

The first line proclaims the beauty, the attraction of the scene
—a line lingering and retarded in its rhythm. But with this statement concerning the attraction—the statement merely gives us
what we have already dramatically arrived at by the fact of the
stopping—we find the repudiation of the attraction. The beauty,
the peace, is a sinister beauty, a sinister peace. It is the beauty
and peace of surrender—the repudiation of action and obligation.
The darkness of the woods is delicious—but treacherous. The
beauty which cuts itself off from action is sterile; the peace which
is a peace of escape is a meaningless and, therefore, a suicidal
peace. There will be beauty and peace at the end of the journey,
in the terms of the fulfillment of the promises, but that will be an
earned beauty stemming from action.

In other words, we have a new contrast here. The fact of the
capacity to stop by the roadside and contemplate the woods sets
man off from the beast, but in so far as such contemplation
involves a repudiation of the world of action and obligation it
cancels the definition of man which it had seemed to establish.
So the poem leaves us with that paradox, and that problem. We
can accept neither term of the original contrast, the poem seems to

say; we must find a dialectic which will accommodate both terms. We must find a definition of our humanity which will transcend both terms.

This theme is one which appears over and over in Frost's poems —the relation, to state the issue a little differently, between the fact and the dream. In another poem, "Mowing," he puts it this way, "The fact is the sweetest dream that labor knows." That is, the action and the reward cannot be defined separately, man must fulfill himself, in action, and the dream must not violate the real. But the solution is not to sink into the brute—to act like the little horse who knows that the farmhouses mean oats—to sink into nature, into appetite. But at the same time, to accept the other term of the original contrast in our poem, to surrender to the pull of the delicious blackness of the woods, is to forfeit the human definition, to sink into nature by another way, a dangerous way which only the human can achieve. So our poem, which is supposed to celebrate nature, may really be a poem about man defining himself by resisting the pull into nature. There are many poems on this subject in Frost's work. In fact, the first poem in his first book is on this subject and uses the same image of the dark wood with its lethal beauty. It is called "Into My Own."

> One of my wishes is that those dark trees,
> So old and firm they scarcely show the breeze,
> Were not, as 'twere, the merest mask of gloom,
> But stretched away until the edge of doom.
>
> I should not be withheld but that some day
> Into their vastness I should steal away,
> Fearless of ever finding open land,
> Or highway where the slow wheel pours the sand.
>
> I do not see why I should e'er turn back,
> Or those should not set forth upon my track
> To overtake me, who should miss me here
> And long to know if still I held them dear.
>
> They would not find me changed from him they
>   knew—
> Only more sure of all I thought was true.

Here the man enters the dark wood but manages to carry his humanity with him; he remains more sure of all he had thought was true. And thus the poem becomes a kind of parable of the

position of the artist, the man who is greatly concerned with the
flux of things, with the texture of the world, with, even, the dark
"natural" places of man's soul. He is greatly concerned with those
things, but he manages to carry over, in terms of those things,
the specifically human.

From "Into My Own" let us turn to a late poem, which again
gives us the man and the dark wood and the invitation to come
into the lethal beauty. This one is called "Come In."

> As I came to the edge of the woods,
> Thrush music—hark!
> Now if it was dusk outside,
> Inside it was dark.
>
> Too dark in the woods for a bird
> By sleight of wing
> To better its perch for the night,
> Though it still could sing.
>
> The last of the light of the sun
> That had died in the west
> Still lived for one song more
> In a thrush's breast.
>
> Far in the pillared dark
> Thrush music went—
> Almost like a call to come in
> To the dark and lament.
>
> But no, I was out for stars:
> I would not come in.
> I meant not even if asked,
> And I hadn't been.

In this woods, too, there is beauty, and an invitation for the
man to come in. And, as in "Stopping by Woods on a Snowy
Evening," he declines the invitation. Let us develop a little more
fully the implications of the contrast between the two poems. The
thrush in the woods cannot now do anything to alter its position.
Practical achievement is at an end—the sleight of wing (a fine
phrase) can do no good. But it still can sing. That is, the darkness
can still be conquered in the very lament. In other words, the poet
is prepared to grant here that a kind of satisfaction, a kind of

conquest, is possible by the fact of expression, for the expression is, in itself, a manifestation of the light which has been withdrawn. Even in terms of the lament, in terms of the surrender to the delicious blackness, a kind of ideal resolution—and one theory of art, for that matter—is possible. (We remember that it was a thing for a man to do and not for a horse to do to stop by the other dark woods.)

But here the man, as before, does not go into the woods. He will not make those terms with his destiny, not, in any case, unless forced to do so. (The thrush cannot do otherwise, but a man can, perhaps, and if he can do otherwise he more fully defines himself as man.) No, the man is out for stars, as he says. Which seems to say that man, by his nature (as distinguished from bird), is not dependent upon the day; he can find in the night other symbols for his aspiration. He will not lament the passing of the day, but will go out for stars.

> I would not come in.
> I meant not even if asked,
> And I hadn't been.

What are we to take as the significance of this last little turn? Is it merely a kind of coyness, a little ironical, wry turn, without content, a mere mannerism? (And in some of Frost's poems we do have the mere mannerism, a kind of self-imitation.) Why had not the man been asked to come in? The thrush's song had seemed to be an invitation. But it had not been an invitation after all. For the bird cannot speak to the man. It has not the language of man. It can speak only in terms of its own world, the world of nature and the dark woods, and not in terms of the man who is waiting for the darkness to define the brilliance of the stars. So here we have again the man-nature contrast (but we must remember that nature is in man, too), the contrast between the two kinds of beauty, and the idea that the reward, the dream, the ideal, stems from action and not from surrender of action.

Let us leave the dark-wood symbol and turn to a poem which, with other materials, treats Frost's basic theme. This is "After Apple-Picking," the poem which I am inclined to think is Frost's masterpiece, it is so poised, so subtle, so poetically coherent in detail.

My long two-pointed ladder's sticking through a tree
Toward heaven still,
And there's a barrel that I didn't fill
Beside it, and there may be two or three
Apples I didn't pick upon some bough.
But I am done with apple-picking now.
Essence of winter sleep is on the night,
The scent of apples: I am drowsing off.
I cannot rub the strangeness from my sight
I got from looking through a pane of glass
I skimmed this morning from the drinking trough
And held against the world of hoary grass.
It melted, and I let it fall and break.
But I was well
Upon my way to sleep before it fell,
And I could tell
What form my dreaming was about to take.
Magnified apples appear and disappear,
Stem end and blossom end,
And every fleck of russet showing clear.
My instep arch not only keeps the ache,
It keeps the pressure of a ladder-round.
I feel the ladder sway as the boughs bend.
And I keep hearing from the cellar bin
The rumbling sound
Of load on load of apples coming in.
For I have had too much
Of apple-picking: I am overtired
Of the great harvest I myself desired.
There were ten thousand thousand fruit to touch,
Cherish in hand, lift down, and not let fall.
For all
That struck the earth,
No matter if not bruised or spiked with stubble,
Went surely to the cider-apple heap
As of no worth.
One can see what will trouble
This sleep of mine, whatever sleep it is.
Were he not gone,
The woodchuck could say whether it's like his
Long sleep, as I describe its coming on,
Or just some human sleep.

The items here—ladder in apple tree, the orchard, drinking trough, pane of ice, woodchuck—all have their perfectly literal meanings—the echo of their meaning in actuality. And the poem, for a while anyway, seems to be commenting on that actual existence those items have. Now, some poems make a pretense of living only in terms of that actuality. For instance, "Stopping by Woods on a Snowy Evening" is perfectly consistent at the level of actuality—a man stops by the woods, looks into the woods, which he finds lovely, dark and deep, and then goes on, for he has promises to keep. It can be left at that level, if we happen to be that literal-minded, and it will make a sort of sense.

However, "After Apple-Picking" is scarcely consistent at the level of actuality. It starts off with a kind of consistency, but something happens. The hero of the poem says that he is drowsing off—and in broad daylight, too. He says that he has a strangeness in his sight which he drew from the drinking trough. So the literal world dissolves into a kind of dream world—the literal world and the dream world overlapping, as it were, like the two sets of elements in a superimposed photograph. What is the nature of this dream world? And what is its relation to the literal world, the world of real apples and the aching instep arch and the real woodchuck?

The poem opens with a few lines which seem to apply wholeheartedly to the literal world:

> My long two-pointed ladder's sticking through a tree
> Toward heaven still,
> And there's a barrel that I didn't fill
> Beside it, and there may be two or three
> Apples I didn't pick upon some bough.

It is all literal enough. We even observe the very literal down-to-earth word "sticking" and the casualness of the tone of the whole passage. In fact, it would be hard to say this more simply than it is said. Even the rhymes are unobtrusive, and all the more so because all of the lines except one are run-on lines. But let us, in the light of the rest of the poem, look more closely. The ladder, we observe, has been left sticking "toward heaven still." That is, as we have said, casual and commonplace enough, but we suddenly realize it isn't merely that, when we remember the poem is about the kind of heaven the poet wants, the kind of dream-after-labor he wants—and expects.

So, to break the matter down into crude statement and destroy the quality of the suggestive-in-the-commonplace, we have a kind of preliminary appearance of the theme which concerns the relation of labor and reward, earth and heaven. With our knowledge of the total poem, we can look back, too, at the next several lines and reread them: Maybe I missed something in my life, in my labor, the poet says, but not much, for I tried quite conscientiously to handle carefully every item of my harvest of experience, to touch with proper appreciation everything that came to hand. Maybe I did miss a few things, he seems to say, but I did the best I could, and on the whole did pretty well.

But now the harvest is over, he says, and the "essence of winter sleep is on the night, the scent of apples." He is aware of the conclusion, the successful conclusion of his effort, and in that awareness there is a strangeness in his sight. He is now looking not into the world of effort but the world of dream, of the renewal. It is misty and strange, as seen through the pane of ice, but still it has the familiar objects of the old world of effort, but the objects now become strange in their very familiarity. He is poised here on the frontier between the two worlds, puzzling about their relationship. But he can already tell, he says, what will be the content of the dream world, the world of reward for labor now accomplished.

> And I could tell
> What form my dreaming was about to take.
> Magnified apples appear and disappear,
> Stem end and blossom end,
> And every fleck of russet showing clear.

The dream will relive the world of effort, even to the ache of the instep arch where the ladder rung was pressed. But is this a cause for regret or for self-congratulation? Is it a good dream or a bad dream? The answer is not to be found in statement, for as far as the statement goes he says:

> For I have had too much
> Of apple-picking: I am overtired
> Of the great harvest I myself desired.

No, we must look for the answer in the temper of the description he gives of the dream—the apples, stem end and blossom end,

and every fleck of russet showing clear. The richness and beauty
of the harvest—magnified now—is what is dwelt upon. In the
dream world every detail is bigger than life, and richer, and can
be contemplated in its fullness. And the accent here is on the word
contemplated. Further, even as the apple picker recalls the details
of labor which made him overtired, he does so in a way which
denies the very statement that the recapitulation in dream will
"trouble" him. For instance, we have the delicious rhythm of the
line,

> I feel the ladder sway as the boughs bend.

It is not the rhythm of nightmare, but of the good dream. Or
we find the same temper in the next few lines in which the poet
returns to the fact that he, in the real world, the world of effort,
had carefully handled and cherished each fruit, and *cherished* is
not the word to use if the labor is mere labor, the brutal act. So
even though we find the poet saying that his sleep will be troubled,
the word *troubled* comes to us colored by the whole temper of the
passage, ironically qualified by that temper. For he would not have
it otherwise than troubled, in this sense.

To quote again:

> One can see what will trouble
> This sleep of mine, whatever sleep it is.
> Were he not gone,
> The woodchuck could say whether it's like his
> Long sleep, as I describe its coming on,
> Or just some human sleep.

Well, what does the woodchuck have to do with it? How does
he enter the poem, and with what credentials? His sleep is con-
trasted with "just some human sleep." The contrast, we see, is on
the basis of the dream. The woodchuck's sleep will be dreamless
and untroubled. The woodchuck is simply in the nature from which
man is set apart. The animal's sleep is the sleep of oblivion. But
man has a dream which distinguishes him from the woodchuck.
But how is this dream related to the literal world, the world of
the woodchuck and apple harvests and daily experience? It is not
a dream which is cut off from that literal world of effort—a heaven
of ease and perpetual rewards, in the sense of rewards as coming
after and in consequence of effort. No, the dream, the heaven, will

simply be a reliving of the effort—magnified apples, stem end and blossom end, and every fleck, every aspect of experience, showing clear.

We have been considering the literal world and the dream world as distinct, for that is the mechanism of the poem, the little myth of the poem. But here it may be well to ask ourselves if the poet is really talking about immortality and heaven—if he is really trying to define the heaven he wants and expects after this mortal life. No, he is only using that as an image for his meaning, a way to define his attitude. And that attitude is an attitude toward the here and now, toward man's conduct of his life in the literal world. So we must make another transliteration.

This attitude has many implications. And this leads us to a rather important point about poetry. When we read a poem merely in terms of a particular application of the attitude involved in it, we almost always read it as a kind of cramped and mechanical allegory. A poem defines an attitude, a basic view, which can have many applications. It defines, if it is a good poem, a sort of strategic point for the spirit from which experience of all sorts may be freshly viewed.

But to return to this poem: What would be some of the implied applications? First, let us take it in reference to the question of any sort of ideal which man sets up for himself, in reference to his dream. By this application the valid ideal would be that which stems from and involves the literal world, which is arrived at in terms of the literal world and not by violation of man's nature as an inhabitant of that literal world. Second, let us take it in reference to man's reward in this literal world. By this application we would arrive at a statement like this: Man must seek his reward in his fulfillment through effort and must not expect reward as something coming at the end of effort, like the oats for the dray horse in the trough at the end of the day's pull. He must cherish each thing in his hand. Third, let us take it in reference to poetry, or the arts. By this application, which is really a variant of the first, we would find that art must stem from the literal world, from the common body of experience, and must be a magnified "dream" of that experience as it has achieved meaning, and not a thing set apart, a mere decoration.

These examples, chosen from among many, are intended merely

to point us back into the poem—to the central impulse of the poem itself. But they are all summed up in this line from "Mowing," another of Frost's poems: "The fact is the sweetest dream that labor knows." However, we can step outside of the poems a moment and find a direct statement from the anti-Platonic Frost. He is comparing himself with E. A. Robinson, but we can see the application to the thematic line which has been emerging in the poems we have been considering.

> I am not the Platonist Robinson was. By Platonist I mean one who believes what we have here is an imperfect copy of what is in heaven. The woman you have is an imperfect copy of some woman in heaven or in someone else's bed. Many of the world's greatest—maybe all of them—have been ranged on that romantic side. I am philosophically opposed to having one Iseult for my vocation and another for my avocation. . . . Let me not sound the least bit smug. I define a difference with proper humility. A truly gallant Platonist will remain a bachelor as Robinson did from unwillingness to reduce any woman to the condition of being used without being idealized.

Smug or not—and perhaps the poet protests his humility a little too much—the passage does give us a pretty clear indication of Frost's position. And the contrast between "vocation" and "avocation" which he uses leads us to another poem in which the theme appears, "Two Tramps in Mud Time." The last stanza is talking about the relation of "love" and "need" as related to an activity—which may be transliterated into "dream" and "fact" if we wish:

> But yield who will to their separation,
> My object in living is to unite
> My avocation and my vocation
> As my two eyes make one in sight.
> Only where love and need are one,
> And the work is play for mortal stakes,
> Is the deed ever really done
> For Heaven and the future's sakes.

And we may notice that we have, in line with our earlier poems on the theme, the apparently contrasting terms "mortal stakes" and "Heaven."

In conclusion, I may cite "Desert Places," which is a late and more bleakly stoical version of "Stopping by Woods on a Snowy Evening," and "Birches," which is almost a variant of "After Apple-Picking." Here are the closing lines of "Birches":

> So was I once myself a swinger of birches.
> And so I dream of going back to be.
> It's when I'm weary of considerations,
> And life is too much like a pathless wood
> Where your face burns and tickles with the cobwebs
> Broken across it, and one eye is weeping
> From a twig's having lashed across it open.
> I'd like to get away from earth awhile
> And then come back to it and begin over.
> May no fate willfully misunderstand me
> And half grant what I wish and snatch me away
> Not to return. Earth's the right place for love:
> I don't know where it's likely to go better.
> I'd like to go by climbing a birch tree,
> And climb black branches up a snow-white trunk
> *Toward* heaven, till the tree could bear no more,
> But dipped its top and set me down again.
> That would be good both going and coming back.
> One could do worse than be a swinger of birches.

For the meaning, in so far as it is abstractly paraphrasable as to theme: Man is set off from nature by that fact that he is capable of the dream, but he is also of nature, and his best dream is the dream of the fact, and the fact is his position of labor and fate in nature though not of her. For the method: The poet has undertaken to define for us both the distinction between and the interpenetration of two worlds, the world of nature and the world of the ideal, the heaven and the earth, the human and the non-human (oppositions which appear in various relationships), by developing images gradually from the literal descriptive level of reference to the symbolic level of reference.

It may be said quite truly in one sense that this interpenetration, this fusion, of the two worlds is inherent in the nature of poetry—that whenever we use a metaphor, even in ordinary conversation, we remark on the interpenetration in so far as our metaphor functions beyond the level of mere mechanical illustration. But the difference between the general fact and these poems is that the interpenetration of the two worlds, in varying ranges of significance, is itself the theme of the poems. We can whimsically say that this does not prove very much. Even the most vindictive Platonist could not do very differently, for in so far as he was bound to state his Platonic theme in words—words, which belong to our world of fact and contingency—he would be unwittingly celebrating the un-Platonic interpenetration of the two worlds.

But there is a practical difference if not an ultimate one. We might get at it this way: The process the poet has employed in all of these poems, but most fully and subtly I think in "After Apple-Picking," is to order his literal materials so that, in looking back upon them as the poem proceeds, the reader suddenly realizes that they have been transmuted. When Shakespeare begins a sonnet with the question, "Shall I compare thee to a summer's day?" and proceeds to develop the comparison, "Thou art more lovely and more temperate," he is assuming the fact of the transmutation, of the interpenetration of the worlds, from the very start. But in these poems, Frost is trying to indicate, as it were, the very process of the transmutation, of the interpenetration. That, and what that implies as an attitude toward all our activities, is the very center of these poems, and of many others among his work.

Nina Baym

An Approach to Robert Frost's Nature Poetry

The reader of Robert Frost's nature lyrics, seeking for their defining qualities, will probably think first of the speaker's unmistakable voice, next of the recurrent rural setting. Most discussions of the lyrics have centered on these aspects. But the speaker has been too quickly assimilated into the tradition of the cracker barrel philosopher, merely because he is colloquial and nonallusive. The setting, simply because it is rural, has often been too facilely assumed to prove that Frost is an antimodern. Instead of examining the poetic landscape in detail, critics have talked about the real New England and Frost's retreat to it. They have labeled Frost a "nature poet" and then assumed that he was a version of Emerson or Wordsworth—as though there were only one way to be a nature poet. In the 1930s, when critical approaches to Frost were developing, this nature poet was rejected by the social critics for being hopelessly old-fashioned, scolded by the humanists for an evasive pantheism and ignored by the new critics because his poems lacked (or seemingly lacked) ironic cross-currents, dissolv-

From *American Quarterly*, XVII (Winter, 1965), 713-23. Published with the permission of the author and the Trustees of the University of Pennsylvania. Copyright, 1965, Trustees of the University of Pennsylvania.

ing potential tension in easy humor. Frost's defenders have too
often accepted the premises of the attacks—that all nature poetry
is of a kind, that a colloquial voice cannot carry tension—and
thereby served mainly to perpetuate the picture of Frost as a sort
of inspired plowman.[1]

In the last decade, close-reading techniques have been applied
to Frost's poetry with exciting and valuable results, but few inter-
preters have escaped entirely the pervasive conviction that to use
nature is to use it in Emersonian or Wordsworthian fashion. If it
is assumed that the use of nature imagery is necessarily tied to
some transcendental doctrine about the correspondence of natural
objects to states or laws of mind, then of course the transcendental
ethic and aesthetic follow, but in a completely circular way. Outer
facts *must* be used to represent inner meanings, and the poem
must celebrate and search for the moment when the barrier
between outer and inner disappears. Phrases such as "outer and
inner weather" and "a boundless moment" may be culled from
Frost's poetry to support this romantic metaphysic, but only
through ignoring the context in which such phrases appear, the
actual details of the rural setting as well as the action which takes
place in that setting.[2]

Similarly, it is too easily assumed that Frost's use of seasonal
imagery necessarily implies a rebirth theme. The very critic who
has calculated the impressive proportion of fall and winter poetry
in the canon, as compared with the scarcity of spring and summer
poetry, has used his own findings against their clear testimony to
argue that rebirth is Frost's major theme.[3] But seasonal imagery
can be used for many purposes, and a poet who hastens all his

---

[1] *Robert Frost: A Collection of Critical Essays,* ed. James M. Cox (Englewood Cliffs, N.J., 1962) contains examples of all these trends. All three lines
of attack have merged recently in the by-now-commonplace assertion that
Frost, for purposes of control, restricts his universe so tightly as to make
its resolutions inapplicable to our world. *E.g.,* George W. Nitchie, *Human
Values in the Poetry of Robert Frost* (Durham, N.C., 1960); Roy Harvey
Pearce, *The Continuity of American Poetry* (Princeton, 1961), pp. 274-83.
[2] Some examples of good criticism with transcendental presuppositions:
Vivian C. Hopkins, "Robert Frost: Out Far and In Deep," *Western Hu-
manities Review,* XIV (Summer, 1960), 247-63; Marion Montgomery, "Robert Frost and His Use of Barriers: Man vs. Nature Towards God," *South
Atlantic Quarterly,* LVII (Summer, 1958), 339-53; William T. Moynihan,
"Fall and Winter in Frost," *Modern Language Notes,* LXXIII (May, 1958),
348-50; John T. Napier, "A Momentary Stay Against Confusion," *Virginia
Quarterly Review* (Summer, 1957), 378-94.
[3] Moynihan, *MLN,* LXXIII, who also notes that most of the rare spring
and summer poems are undercut by end-season imagery.

seasons toward an inevitable and almost perpetual winter is not talking about spring.

The way out of this dilemma is to abandon the approach to Frost through ideological preconceptions, and to put the poet not in a tradition of thought, but in a specifically "poetic" tradition. Such an approach has been taken most illuminatingly by Lynen and by Brower. Their books, despite quite different emphases, find that both Frost's subject and his methods derive from his conviction that poetry is a unique discipline with its own characteristic subject matters as well as its own uses of language.[4]

Frost, in the long "public poems" (Brower's phrase) which seem designed as defenses of the main corpus of his work, says this himself. When, in "New Hampshire," he responds to the demand that he choose to be a prude or puke by evasion—"me for the hills where I don't have to choose" (p. 210)—he is not making a declaration of retreat from the contemporary.[5] He is resisting the attempt of the New York poet to confine him within arbitrary and limited boundaries which cut him off from his special task and subject as poet. "It seems a narrow choice the age insists on" (p. 211). Running to the hills, Frost is moving toward the poet's theme, a theme which city poets avoid not because it is out of date, but because they are afraid of it. This theme Frost calls "flux." The city poet "had a special terror of the flux/ That showed itself in dendrophobia" (pp. 210-11). This poet may rationalize his rejection of nature as a rejection of the irrelevant, but Frost believes that he is really covering up the paralyzing fear he feels when confronting "flux."

In "Build Soil" Frost repeats the idea that he uses the rural landscape to fulfill his commitments to the "poetic" theme. As he refused, in "New Hampshire," to write urban poetry, he refuses here to write agrarian poetry. His purpose in using nature is not to be political or topical, and he will not "advertise our farms to city buyers/ Or else write something to improve food prices" (p. 421). He denies that the times have

> "reached a depth
> Of desperation that would warrant poetry's

---

[4] John Lynen, *The Pastoral Art of Robert Frost* (New Haven, 1960); Reuben Brower, *The Poetry of Robert Frost: Constellations of Intention* (New York, 1963).
[5] References to Frost's poetry, given in the text, are to the *Complete Poems of Robert Frost* (New York, 1949).

> Leaving love's alternation, joy and grief,
> The weather's alternation, summer and winter,
> Our age-long theme" (p. 422).

Poetry's special subject, called "flux" in New Hampshire, is here called "alternation." If we give the theme its age-long name, "mutability," we have to recognize the truth in Frost's contention.[6]

This division between love's alternations and the weather's alternations corresponds roughly to the two types of poetry (excluding the apologetics) which are the bulk of Frost's work. First, we have the pastoral dialogues, eclogues and monologues dealing with the mutability of human relations and human existence. Among these we find poems about the severing of ties of life ("Out, Out,—"), of limb ("The Self-Seeker"), of youth, pride and beauty ("The Lovely Shall be Choosers," "Two Witches"), of love ("The Hill Wife," "The Housekeeper"), even of grief ("Home Burial").

Second, we have the nature lyrics, usually composed as tiny dramas of recognition, illumination or resolution involving a lone speaker confronting the landscape. In these poems, the landscape demonstrates the fact of mutability incessantly and obviously, forcing the speaker into reaction. In these poems, Frost shares with Emerson nothing more than the assumption that nature can be used to uncover and illustrate the underlying laws of the universe, because it operates by such laws. Ultimately, Frost's approach to nature is more scientific than Emersonian, for Frost does not take Emerson's next step, to insist that the laws of outer nature correspond to the laws of inner mind. Without this step there is no arriving at a transcendental absorption into nature.

Emerson himself recognized clearly that none of his statements about nature proved the doctrine of correspondences; he only maintained that it was a possible way of looking at the world, and on which was particularly congenial to human wishes. This justified, to him, taking it for true. "The advantage," he said in the "Idealism" section of *Nature*, "of the ideal theory over the popular faith is this, that it presents the world in precisely that view which is most desirable to the mind." But desirability is far from justification for Frost. On the contrary, this is the danger signal which

---

[6] Radcliffe Squires, *Major Themes of Robert Frost* (Ann Arbor, 1963), p. 38, mentions mutability as a theme in Frost's poetry, but does not explore the idea. Committed to a view of Frost as a transcendentalist, although a somewhat shaky one, the author sees Frost as attempting on the whole to deny or overcome or hide the vision of nature which he sees. But I would argue that the poems involve a confronting of the fact of mutability.

calls for re-examination. He considers and resolves very early in his poetry the question of whether "correspondences" or any other version of the pathetic fallacy is a valid approach to nature, and answers negatively. The New England landscape reveals only the laws of the natural world.

Why then, one might ask, does Frost care about these laws? Isn't purely natural truth the province of the scientist? If nature reveals no human truth, why write poetry about it? Questions such as these lie beneath the insistence of most critics that Frost's approach to nature is somehow transcendental. But the answer is that of course Frost is interested in the human truth of nature; yet such truth need not be transcendental. Man wants to know the laws of the world he lives in precisely because it is the world *he* lives in. He can act meaningfully in it only if he understands it. If there are correspondences, he should know this; if there are not, he should know that, and he should not then act as if there were. And the laws which Frost's investigations uncover force him to abandon, regretfully, the transcendental position. For he does not find in nature a transcendental unity or an assurance of rebirth, but rather the grim laws of change and decay.

The poem "A Boundless Moment" with its teasing transcendental title, provides an epitome of the process of rejecting wishful thinking about nature for a more somber truth (p. 288). It describes what seems a glimpse of promise and delight in nature. Walking in the woods in March, the speaker and a friend sight something white through the trees. It looks like flowers, and suggests May with all its connotations of spring, hope, rebirth. " 'Oh, that's the Paradise-in-bloom,' I said."

But truth, with all its matter of fact, breaks in. Though it is pretty to imagine this white something to be May flowers, so hopefully named, the speaker and his friend cannot remain in this "strange world" they know to be false. They must reject a May interpretation when they know it is March. The interpretation of the mystery is "a young beech clinging to its last year's leaves."

This reality is not symbolically neutral. The substitution of a beech clothed in dead leaves for paradise-in-bloom effectively replaces images of spring with images of autumn, images of birth with those of death. Spring flowers viewed through the blurred vision of hope and wish turn to dead leaves when the eyes focus. The story recounted in "A Boundless Moment" dramatizes the movement of man's mind away from a comforting illusion toward a harsh truth. The cyclic seasonal imagery which has so often provided poets with symbols of faith and hope is here manipulated to suggest a movement which culminates in death. Insofar as man is part of the natural order, he is part of a system of perpetual waste and decay. What hope there is for man, what faith he may develop, cannot be based on the assumption that nature tends toward renewal and regeneration.

The recognition of and reaction to mutability constitute in a great number of cases the "action" in a Frost nature lyric. The channel for conveying the knowledge of mutability is nature, usually in autumn or winter, but occasionally in spring or summer. Moynihan has calculated that almost one-third of Frost's total output uses fall and winter imagery (see note 2). Among fall and winter poems are some of the poet's most famous—"Stopping by Woods on a Snowy Evening," "Desert Places," "The Wood Pile," "An Old Man's Winter Night," "After Apple Picking," "The Onset," "The Strong Are Saying Nothing," "I Will Sing You One O," "Bereft," to name a few. The idea of mutability in such poems is conveyed not only in their late season settings, but by the details which emphasize the inevitable and ceaseless movement toward death—night fall, leaf fall, snow fall. Fall in Frost's poetry is less a static season than a process which continues through all seasons, signifying the movement toward death.

Much the greater number of the occasional spring and summer poems are also poems about "fall" in this sense. I have found only one spring poem which is entirely affirmative, "Putting in the Seed." In the typical spring poems, like "Nothing Gold Can Stay," dawn goes down, or falls, to day, reminding us in its beauty mainly of its transience (p. 212). Spring pools, in earliest spring reflecting the sky "almost without defect," will "like the flowers beside them soon be gone," drunk up by roots, turned into leaves which "darken nature" (p. 303). Summer is a time to mourn the lost spring and to wait, resignedly, the certain approach of autumn. The purple fringed flower is sought for and found, but the discovery means only that "summer was done" (p. 459). The ovenbird, from the darkened mid-summer wood, recalls the petal fall and heralds that "other fall" (p. 150).

Though Frost never hesitates to infer from spring and summer the certain coming of winter, he is not correspondingly ready to affirm from winter the certain return of spring. "The strong are saying nothing until they see" spring return with their own eyes (p. 391). And in "The Onset," that perplexing poem, even though the poet avers "I know that winter death has never tried/ The earth but it has failed," he cannot commit himself entirely to an affirmation. When all the white snow is gone from the earth, a few white objects around will still wear the color of mortality—a birch, for example, symbolizing (as trees usually do in Frost's poetry) natural life which is always necessarily obedient to universal law; and some houses and a church, symbols almost certainly for human life (p. 278).

Occasional gleams in this darkening universe serve only to make the darkness visible, as in "An Old Man's Winter Night" (p. 135). White is usually the color of death, especially as associated with snow. At times it signifies indifference, especially when connected with the stars (p. 12). And occasionally it is used as Melville uses it to mean an enticing but unfathomable truth, perhaps delusory. The white beech in "A Boundless Moment" is an example of this; so is the mysterious white something in "For Once, Then, Something," which may be truth, or perhaps a pebble of quartz (p. 275). The moon in "Acquainted With the Night" proclaims nothing relevant to man, only that the "time is neither wrong nor right" (p. 324), and falling snow in "Desert Places" has "no expression, nothing to express" (p. 386).

To this traditional imagery Frost has added a whole new vocabulary of metaphor drawn from scientific law, and thereby perhaps shown himself to be the one modern poet for whom scientific truth is not necessarily at odds with poetry. Radcliffe Squires has presented a reading of "West Running Brook" based on the Second Law of Thermodynamics, a law familiar in the literary context because Henry Adams selected it to explain history.[7] But despite some startling coincidences of imagery in Frost's poems with some images used by William James in corresponding on the Second Law with Adams (the correspondence is detailed by Squires), it is not likely that Frost found the law here. This is because Adams used it metaphorically to explain human history, while Frost leaves the law in context and uses it where it belongs, to explain nature.

This law simply says that the amount of disorder in the universe is continually increasing. In our universe, heat cannot of itself flow from a cold to a hot body; the movement of heat is always in one direction. It can never go backward, and thus our universe is an "irreversible system." Since the predominant temperature of our universe is cold, the predominant direction of heat flow is from

---

[7] Squires, p. 103.

individual bodies out into their environment, and as the temperature of the body approaches that of its environment (in our world, cools) it runs down, stops working. The process being irreversible, is one of a universe getting increasingly rundown, increasingly disorderly.

It is quite clear that Frost uses this law consciously in his poetry as a source of metaphor, for there are passages which refer to it unmistakably. In "The Wood Pile," for example, the pile itself provides an almost classic illustration of the law as it is left to "warm the frozen swamp/ With the slow, smokeless burning of decay" (p. 126). Job, discoursing with God in "A Masque of Reason," rejects Dante's view of the universe as a circular or reversible process where "rays return upon themselves," insisting "I hold rays deteriorate to nothing,/ First white, then red, then ultra-red, then out" (p. 601). In "West Running Brook," the man makes a parallel contrast between a view of the world as static, and his own view of the world running down.

> "Some say existence . . .
> Stands still and dances, but it runs away.
> It seriously, sadly, runs away,
> To fill the abyss' void with emptiness" (p. 328).

The movement of the universe is the "universal cataract of death/ That spends to nothingness" (p. 329).

We are not dealing here with a modernized version of the golden age myth. The cataract is the eternal condition of existence itself. There never was a time in the created life of anything when that life was not running down. New life is continually coming into being, new dawns are dawning, new springs springing, but the instant of springing is the beginning of the fall. This idea is carried mainly in the image of the cataract (ironically but obviously associated with springtime) and appears in such poems as "One Step Backward Taken," where the whole world goes plunging down the gully (p. 519) and in "The Master Speed" where existence is characterized as the "rush of everything to waste" (p. 392). And the underlying winter and night metaphor in Frost's poetry is a metaphor for a world both cold and chaotic, a world wasted and run down.

In such a world, what possible meaningful action can man perform? In a word, he can resist. That heat or energy with which the human being is endowed by being created, the losing of which is the inevitable progress of his life toward age and death, should be spent and can be spent in a "backward motion towards the source," refusing to cooperate with the downward rush (p. 329). Frost's word for the power which enables man to direct his portion of energy from "the one time and only the one/ When dust really took in the sun" (p. 342), is "mind." The hostile sea of "Sand Dunes" does not know mankind if "by any change of shape/ She hopes to cut off mind" (p. 330).

Mind is the uniquely human characteristic, and man defines himself therefore as man by asserting it against the push of matter. This mind, in "All Revelation," by probing, discovering, learning nature, in a sense creates it (p. 444); but on the final question of whether the existence of human mind implies purpose in the universe, whether the human mind stands in some relation to a divine mind, if there is a divine mind—on all such final or teleological questions Frost is consistently uncommitted.

Many critics have called Frost anti-intellectual or intellectually limited because of this lack of teleology, or because he tends to regard teleological systems with suspicion. Implicit in such criticism is the common view that there is only one way to be truly "intellectual," which is to be teleological, to talk about purpose in the universe. Frost seems rather to have decided, seriously and sincerely, that questions about purpose cannot be answered, and that man must therefore make his way without guessing at final causes. He is therefore, in the view of many, a writer of what can only be minor poetry.

The most extreme statement of this view, though it is to be found commonly in Frost criticism, occurs in Nitchie's *Human Values in the Poetry of Robert Frost* (see note 1), p. 209. Here the author maintains that it is far more profound and intellectual to adopt a patently absurd cosmology like Yeats' so long as one is thereby enabled to order the universe teleologically, than to hold fast to uncertainty and attempt to write good poetry without the scaffolding of a myth one cannot believe. To the notion that to be profound is to be teleological, Frost counters that to be profound is to be true to the results of one's thought and observation of the universe. This is the extent of his anti-intellectualism, for he is otherwise a persistent celebrant of the power and glory of the human mind.

Hence, even though he celebrates resistance, he does not thereby imply that there is something to be recovered or some place to return to. The utopian dream of "The Lost Follower" (p. 483) and the nostalgic quest for Eden in "Directive" are alike delusory, because they assume a static period. But the assumption in Frost's poetry is that in creation there has been no stasis; only in death is there stillness. We go back, in "Directive," to discover only ruins; crumbled fragments are all we get of wholeness (p. 520). The home of timeless truths, in "The Black Cottage," is a "desert . . . walled/ By mountain ranges half in summer snow,/ Sand dunes held loosely in tamarask" (p. 77). In a world where all is rushing to chaos, no permanent recovery or journey back would be possible, and the timeless spot one aimed for either in the past or in the future would prove to be illusion. Return to the past is thus doubly impossible: it cannot be done, and it was never there. And Frost's notions of human action are strongly constrained by his grim requirement that they be limited to the possible.

The most a man can do is by continued resistance to hold his ground. Like the west running brook, his achievement will be a white wave "not gaining but not losing" (p. 328). The human action in Frost's poetry is a repeated gesture of defiance, a countless succession of moments of resistance, each of which is, in Frost's wonderfully apt phrase, "a momentary stay against confusion."

The poems are full of such gestures of stay, transient but affirmative within realistic limits. Such gestures constitute the action in many of Frost's little lyric dramas. Brown, having lost his footing in a dark and icy world, and slipped down two miles of mountainside, sets off back home, undaunted by the hour, the climb or the fact that he has to go miles out of his way to get back up (pp. 173-75). The brook of "West Running Brook" runs back against the source, and so is a good symbol for man, as is the moon which stays the spring thaw in "A Hillside Thaw" (p. 293). In "One Step Backward Taken," it is, as the title implies, a step back which saves the speaker from plunging down into chaos (p. 519). The unknown woodsman in "The Wood Pile" has left a human mark in that random wood where the view is "all in lines/ Straight up and down of tall slim trees/ Too much alike to mark or name a place by." The expense of his energy into that no-where has made it somewhere, has left the organized and ordered wood pile as the symbol of man's desire to make order out of the chaos of his environment. Having stacked his wood, he has turned on to fresh tasks, suggesting perhaps that it is less the achievement than the gesture of ordering which interests Frost. And this interest may stem from Frost's belief that the achievement of order is necessarily temporary; the wood pile is now warming the frozen swamp "with the slow smokeless burning of decay" (p. 126).

The speaker in "The Master Speed" wishes for the couple "in the rush of everything to waste/ That you may have the power of standing still" (p. 392). The isolated, grim lives which figure so frequently in Frost's poetry all exhibit that power which, in one poem, Frost most significantly calls "staying" (p. 337). All planting, building, tilling, chopping, linelaying—all such acts are human acts of ordering chaos. One of the most famous of such acts in Frost's poetry is mending wall. It becomes increasingly clear, as more critics work on the poem, that the wall-mending is not being condemned by the speaker.[8] The speaker criticizes his neighbor for not asking *why* they build or mend walls. He cooperates with, even initiated, the mending process itself. The wall is mended as a gesture, annually repeated, against that "something" that "doesn't love a wall,/ That wants it down." Together, the speaker and his neighbor are engaged in the fundamental human enterprise, making a momentary stand against the principle of confusion that "spills the upper boulders in the sun" (p. 47).

"Stopping By Woods on a Snowy Evening" provides another example. Here the speaker struggles against and overcomes the temptation to go along with the flood, to get swept into the inevitable course of nature. He turns a resolute back on the loveliness of dark woods and cold snow, picks up the reins and returns to his promises (p. 275). "Come In" is another version of the same story. The poet at the edge of the woods in a dark world resists the invitation of the bird to go into the still greater dark and lament. He resists, too, in the poem's final line, the temptation to read the world as inviting him to anything. He is out for stars, and he maintains his quest in the face of darkness and indifference (p. 446). The leaf treader, in the poem so named, rejects a similar invitation extended by the falling leaves, stamping them underfoot.

> "They spoke to the fugitive in my heart as if it were leaf to leaf.
> They tapped at my eyelids and touched my lips with an invitation
>   to grief.
> But it was no reason I had to go because they had to go.
> Now up to my knees to keep on top of another year of snow"
> (p. 388).

The aim in Frost's poetry is to develop a human act which has meaning in terms of the world man really lives in. The first step is

---

[8] See John C. Broderick, *Explicator,* XIV, item 24 (Jan. 1956) and Carson Gibb, *Explicator,* XX, item 48 (Feb. 1962).

to find out what kind of world it really is. The world Frost discovers, and he depicts the making of this discovery in many nature lyrics, is not friendly to man's great hopes, dreams and needs. But to despair in it is *not* the human answer to the grim world discovered. To be glum, as Frost says in "The Times Table," is the best way "To close a road, abandon a farm,/ Reduce the births of the human race,/ And bring back nature in people's place" (p. 336).

On the other hand, grandiose, sustained or programmatic actions are not the answer either, for this is a world in which such actions can be initiated only through blindness or willful self-deception, neither of which states accords with Frost's picture of "mind." What is possible is the small gesture, which, however, must be unremittingly repeated. The human life is not heroic in an epic sense. It is a life of staying.

This solution is certainly not transcendental. This is not a life in conformity with nature, nor a life striving to be merged into nature. On the contrary, it is rather an endless battle against the decaying flux which nature, lacking mind, is continually victim to and therefore continually illustrates. Because the flux endures as long as existence endures, the battle against it is endless.

Not the least of possible human actions is the poem. In "The Aim Was Song," man converts the natural and chaotic wind into song by *holding* it in his mouth long enough to *reverse* its direction, to convert north into south. The result is song, thus demonstrated to be a defiance of natural process (p. 274). In "The Grindstone," too, the blade is sharpened by overcoming the pressure exerted on the stone by a "father time-like man," by an act against the easy direction (p. 232). The body of ideas in the poetry and the kind of poetry written thus coincide. Frost's poems are examples of the one kind of action, mind staying flux, which he recognizes as meaningfully asserting the human in a fundamentally nonhuman world.

William H. Pritchard

Diminished Nature

I

The figure a poem makes. It begins in delight and ends in wisdom. . . . It begins in delight, it inclines to the impulse, it assumes direction with the first line laid down, it runs a course of lucky events, and ends in a clarification of life—not necessarily a great clarification, such as sects and cults are founded on, but in a momentary stay against confusion.

No matter how many times we hear this oft-quoted statement of Frost's, the final clause pulls us up short for contemplation. This, we feel, is a distinctive and individual way to talk about what poems do. Instead of assuring us that poetry is, after all, the highest form of knowledge, or a priceless heritage we can ill afford to neglect, or even an unparaphrasable union of form and content, Frost gives us the term "clarification"—and "not necessarily a great clarification" at that. Yet despite his unwillingness to make

From *The Massachusetts Review,* I (Spring, 1960), 475-92. Reprinted from *The Massachusetts Review* © 1960 The Massachusetts Review, Inc.

large claims for what clarification involves, the phrase "momentary stay against confusion" tips us off. Whether we choose to emphasize the poem as "stay" (he speaks elsewhere in the preface of a "line of purpose" struck across "experience"), or to stress its limited momentariness, or to underline the "confusion" against which the poem stands and which it partially orders, we get a sense that Frost thinks of poetry as a precarious game played in the face of peril—"the vast chaos of all I have lived through"— and for that reason a game absolutely necessary to play. In the words of "The Road Not Taken" ". . . that has made all the difference": through poetry we distinguish ourselves from the chaos of experience by striking "a line of purpose across it for somewhere."

Looking at the *Complete Poems*, we are struck, particularly in the lyrics and shorter narratives, by a correspondence between what Frost says a poem should do and the kind of dramatic situations his poems enact. Perhaps this is not surprising; we assume that like most poets Frost did not begin with a definition of poetry but instead wrote poems. When it came time to preface his complete works the definition grew out of a lifetime of verse, and to say that a particular poem conforms to or bears out his large definition of poetry would not be of much critical use. The relationship between individual poems and Frost's definition of poetry is more intimate and complicated than terms like "conforming to" or "bearing out" suggest; it is necessary to make a distinction between the Frost for whom the writing of each poem is a "momentary stay against confusion" and the various speakers of these poems, each of whom faces an analogous threat and attempts to make his own stay.

The relationship becomes even more interesting when, within the poem, not only the speaker but his subject—the person or object contemplated and talked about—is occupied with working out such a stay. In a poem like "An Old Man's Winter Night" we can distinguish three such efforts: the actions and gestures of the aged man who shores up fragments against a threatening environment; the speaker's attempt to comment on these actions in a sympathetic, faithful and unsentimental way—to make a verbal stay that is just adequate; and finally the relationship among environment, old man, and speaker—the stay of form which is the poem itself.

The tenuous adequacy felt in a definition of poetry as "a momentary stay against confusion" is found in the experience dealt

with in many of Frost's poems. A large group of them can be
classified as poems about deprivation or loss; that is, the experience which is the subject of these poems is characteristically
viewed as limited in its range, thoroughly conditioned by circumstances and somewhat less than fully satisfying in its value to the
speaker. The contradiction that appears throughout these poems
is of experience as it is imagined, remembered or longed for—full,
exhilarating, unbounded—and experience as it is felt—partial,
painful, limited. This is certainly not an unusual contradiction for
poets to regard—as Wordsworth, Shelley and Keats remind us;
but one of Frost's distinctions as a poet is that he takes the contradiction seriously and provides us with some fresh ways of
meeting it. A look at three familiar poems which feature some
stock objects of nineteenth century English verse—birds, brooks
and rural matters in general—will serve to point up Frost's difference from his romantic predecessors. In a preface to his play "A
Way Out" Frost asserts that "everything written is as good as it
is dramatic"; this assertion can be reconciled with his insistence
that the poem "ends in wisdom" by paying particular attention to
the quality of wisdom that is achieved.

II

> There is a singer everyone has heard,
> Loud, a mid-summer and a mid-wood bird,
> Who makes the solid tree trunks sound again.
> He says that leaves are old and that for flowers
> Mid-summer is to spring as one to ten.
> He says the early petal-fall is past,
> When pear and cherry bloom went down in showers
> On sunny days a moment overcast;
> And comes that other fall we name the fall.
> He says the highway dust is over all.
> The bird would cease and be as other birds
> But that he knows in singing not to sing.
> The question that he frames in all but words
> Is what to make of a diminished thing.

"The Oven Bird" is one of Frost's finest poems, yet the reader who
comes upon it for the first time is not struck by any surprisingly
dramatic features. All the lines, except for the second, are fairly

regular; there are no outstanding changes in tone—even the wry joke about the "fall" has to be delivered with about the same inflection as the opening line; nor do the images present any difficulty or demand special attention. Yet the poem is distinguished in its use of language and rightness of tone. By expressing the "diminished thing" in a language which the bird "all but" uses, the poem creates a remarkable decorum, an appropriateness of words to theme that is perhaps its chief pleasure.

This decorum establishes, almost insinuates, itself in the casual assumed manner of its opening assertion: "There is a singer everyone has heard." The bird exists not as a special discovery of the speaker's or as a product of any particular time or place. Unlike the sudden appearance of the darkling thrush in Hardy's poem: "At once a voice arose among/The bleak twigs overhead," the oven bird just "is"; accordingly Frost's speaker has no particular needs, is not engaged in anything, it would seem, except conveying some information about the bird to anyone who will listen. In fact the voice we hear sounds like a good naturalist who does not try to put anything over on the reader but trusts that reportorial accuracy about his specimen will suffice. The repeated "He says" carries on a deadpan recitation of the bird's message and effects a neat balance among considerations of present, past and future scenes: the oven bird details a present nature which is sparsely populated, refers to the lush "early petal fall" he has seen, and predicts the even scantier future in which "the highway dust is over all." We also notice the frequency with which the verb "is" recurs to designate existence, identity and ratio; this frequent use of "is" in preference to active verbs contributes to the insinuated decorum. Nothing actually happens within the poem; rather the static, ordered conditions about which the bird sings are calmly set before us by a speaker whose own saying is as cautious and knowing as the subject of the poem.

This closeness between speaker and bird—the correspondences between a diminished natural scene, a specially appropriate song and the speaker's decorous rendering of both, is Frost's way of inverting the romantic relationship between a poet beset by tribulations, and an object (frequently a bird) whose condition is seen as admirably opposite to his own. Shelley's skylark is not a bird but a symbol of full spontaneous life: "Hail to thee, blithe Spirit!/ Bird thou never wert," and he invokes it in the highest style, unqualified by any doubt or irony: "Thou lovest—but ne'er knew

love's sad satiety." The bird has all the qualities of human life
without sharing any of its defects and uncertainties. As opposed
to this "crystal stream" of song

> We look before and after,
>   And pine for what is not:
> Our sincerest laughter
>   With some pain is fraught;
> Our sweetest songs are those that tell of saddest thought.

Shelley exults in the disparity between the skylark and humanity,
for it allows him at the end of the poem to cry enthusiastically,
"Teach me half thy gladness," a plea that he as a special human
being—a poet—may be magically singled out and infused with
superhuman qualities. The gap between joyous freedom and painful limitation can be closed by the speaker's fervent prayer.

Keeping in mind this brief definition of a romantic convention
we can see how Hardy's "The Darkling Thrush" stands half-way
between Shelley and Frost in its treatment of this convention.
Hardy's landscape bears analogies to the scant mid-summer scene
of "The Oven Bird" and his speaker feels perfectly in tune with
the deprived circumstances: "The ancient pulse of germ and birth/
Was shrunken hard and dry,/And every spirit upon earth/Seemed
fervorless as I." At exactly the moment when the "I" makes a
connection between his fervorless state and the nature around him,
something happens which partially disrupts the correspondence.
The aged thrush sings out with full-voiced joy and forces the
speaker to reexamine the neat, if joyless, analogy he has made:

> So little cause for carolings
>   Of such ecstatic sound
> Was written on terrestrial things
>   Afar or nigh around,
>
> That I could think there trembled through
>   His happy good-night air
> Some blessed Hope, whereof he knew
>   And I was unaware.

The state of these "terrestrial things" is similar to the scene in
which the oven bird sings, but the thrush produces "ecstatic
sound." The dramatic interest of the poem, then, lies in the way
the speaker will take this caroling; since everything on earth is

not so fervorless as he himself, his joyless identification with the scene has been disturbed. But while Shelley ends his poem with a rapturous plea to the skylark, Hardy does not attempt to close the gap between himself and the caroling bird. The thrush is, after all, aged and gaunt; his "happy good-night air" may well be his own farewell to terrestrial things, and the language with which the speaker makes his "stay" properly takes this into account in its cautious grammar and moderate tone. The "Hope" which trembles through the bird's song is purposely left vague and unspecified—the capital letter sets it off as a very large abstraction. Whatever the nature of such Hope, the speaker is extremely guarded in his statement of what it can mean to him. "That I could think . . ." certainly presents the minimum argument for belief. The conditional permissive tense takes us one remove from any actual thinking and at least suggests the possibility that the thrush's song may be, at most, a momentarily pleasing self-deception.

There can be no large dramatic moment of recognition in "The Oven Bird" since Frost's speaker does not ask us to be interested in his situation. His minimum claim for the meaning of the bird's song is in accord with the latter's own unextravagant celebration of experience. Nor does the scene itself ask to be celebrated; in fact

> The bird would cease and be as other birds
> But that he knows in singing not to sing.
> The question that he frames in all but words
> Is what to make of a diminished thing.

The preceding lines with their evocations of "fall" and "all" might seem obvious prey for talk about Edenic overtones, yet the very bald and amusing play on "fall" deflates any solemn symbolic interpretation. The speaker explains the bird's persistence in song by means of a paradox that is not easily translatable but whose meaning seems clear. The oven bird is able to persist in song because, in effect, he is not taken in by it. Such singing has to be unillusioned, looking backwards with regret and forward without vain hope. The bird ". . . knows in singing not to sing": his song is so unlike that of other birds (it is carried on alone and at the wrong time) that it is not song as Shelley's lark was capable of; yet it celebrates nature and experience, however ruefully and guardedly, and it is able to do this by looking on deprivation, imagining still more to come and thus refusing to be overwhelmed.

In an earlier poem, "Reluctance," Frost's speaker confronts the
dying nature of late fall and asks, "Ah, when to the heart of man/
Was it ever less than a treason/To go with the drift of things."
The oven bird's "stay," like the heart's question, is a protest
against the drift of things; since the bird knows exactly what the
fall will be like it uses this knowledge and "frames in all but
words" a question that is its own answer. The reader, like the
speaker, does not try to answer this question by going beyond
the limits it defines. In "Mowing," the whispering of the scythe
communicates no secret to the mower but simply expresses the
sound of its own activity: "The fact is the sweetest dream that
labor knows." So the oven bird's wise persistence in song is the
question that he frames—the "what" of the concluding line.

This poem is a good example of how Frost poetically confronts
deprivation, the "diminished thing," by insisting upon the fact.
Such insistence is perfectly imaged through the bird who makes
song out of the very conditions which would seemingly deny that
song and make it inappropriate. What I call the decorum of pres-
entation—the way in which the speaker relays the bird's song to
us, then accounts for its occurrence without changing his tone of
diction—creates something like a "middle style" which we take
pleasure in. "The Darkling Thrush" carries the romantic situation
of fervorless man confronting joyous bird to one sort of culmina-
tion. In a joyless universe, a man can still be momentarily surprised by joy, but he can not relate the occurrence to anything in
his own experience. Although he may speak of "some blessed
Hope," his very way of phrasing places it well outside his consciousness; that the poem ends with "unaware" is not an accident.
Frost restylizes the situation by humanizing the bird, giving it that
ability to look before and after which Shelley had lamented as the
unfortunate burden of mankind. The "diminished thing" can be
celebrated by a certain kind of singing; it is this knowledge that
the oven bird and the speaker share, and that we experience by
reading the poem.

Frost's poetry dramatizes what can be made of diminished
things. Consider "Hyla Brook," a related companion piece to "The
Oven Bird":

> By June our brook's run out of song and speed.
> Sought for much after that, it will be found
> Either to have gone groping underground

(And taken with it all the Hyla breed
That shouted in the mist a month ago,
Like ghost of sleigh-bells in a ghost of snow)—
Or flourished and come up in jewelweed,
Weak foliage that is blown upon and bent,
Even against the way its waters went.
Its bed is left a faded paper sheet
Of dead leaves stuck together by the heat—
A brook to none but who remember long.
This as it will be seen is other far
Than with brooks taken otherwere in song.
We love the things we love for what they are.

We are presented with another stock poetic object which does not behave in the accustomed way. The oven bird cannot "be as other birds" because of the special knowledge it possesses, but Hyla Brook is more pathetically unable to keep up appearances—a diminished thing that can make no claim for itself. It falls to the speaker then to see what can be made of it; he must know in singing not to sing or else any claim he makes will be ridiculous and inappropriate.

The opening line strikes a familiar straightforward note. The facts about what happens to "our brook" will be set forth without hesitation, and the studied casualness of "sought for much after that" confirms a disarmingly offhand manner with which the brook's plight is registered. The alternative situations in which the brook may be "found" are equally pathetic: either it has disappeared underground, leaving but a mysterious echo of former sounds, or it has ironically "flourished" by merging with the jewelweed which only obstructs its flow; thus both "song and speed" are things of the past, available only to those who "remember long." With the melancholy "A brook to none but who remember long" a reader might feel that he has sensed the poem's direction and anticipated the elegiac note on which it will surely end; the line, in its wistfully inverted syntax assures him that he, like the thoughtful speaker, can triumph over the diminished present by invoking remembrance of things past. Thus the remainder of the poem comes as a shock which unsettles expectation:

This as it will be seen is other far
Than with brooks taken otherwere in song.
We love the things we love for what they are.

The slightly annoyed irregularity of the two lines before the last disturbs the even calm of "A brook to none but who remember long" and its apparent satisfactions with the consolations of memory. "This as it will be seen" refers back to the particular Hyla Brook described but also to the speaker's whole manner of celebration—his own way of seeing this unlikely brook. The reference to other brooks is probably Frost's sly distancing of his treatment from Tennyson's babbler—"For men may come and men may go/But I go on for ever." At any rate, the kind of song which this speaker rejects is similar to what the oven bird avoided by knowing in singing not to sing; the fact that Hyla Brook has so clearly "run out of song" determines the way it should be "taken in song" by this particular speaker. This way is boldly and clearly set forth in the extra line which caps the sonnet and the regularity of whose ten word measure strikes both eye and ear with its annunciation. The love implied by the oven bird's persistent question —"what to make of a diminished thing"—is directly invoked as this speaker's way of taking the brook; both of them love the things they love "for what they are."

This final line substitutes a loving contemplation of the diminished thing for the earlier appeal to memory: "what they are" takes precedence over past glories of what they have been. Frost's willingness to end this poem and many others with a statement rather than an image seems to some readers a serious failing of his art, a refusal to carry out his own principle that every poem written is as good as it is dramatic." A. Alvarez has complained that in too many poems "There is a refusal to let be, a refusal to allow the reader to do a little of the creative work for himself." He goes on to argue that "Frost's insistence on his meaning is to poetry what the over-use of italics is to prose—more of an irritation than a help."[1] Such insistence on the meaning is annoying because it hands over to the reader the right way to feel about this or that experience; Alvarez makes a legitimate criticism which could be applied to certain of Frost's poems, but it is important to see why it is inapplicable to "Hyla Brook." Our interest in this poem does not consist solely in how we should feel about the faded subject but also in how the speaker will dramatically reveal his way of taking it. And "dramatic" is the right word to describe the movement in the last four lines, emphasizing as it does the distance from

[1] *The Shaping Spirit: Studies in Modern English and American Poets* (London, 1958), 170.

where the speaker starts out to where he ends. We do not hear the philosopher dispensing homely wisdom and irritatingly "doing the work for us" but a speaker faced with a particular situation and redefining his manner of taking it. "Hyla Brook" is a representative Frost poem in that it "ends in wisdom," but wisdom is something other than the poet's doling out of an unassailable truth, for it invokes a sense of what has been rejected by the final determined statement. The wisdom of this poem is inseparable from the way Frost's speaker works out his momentary stay not by assertion but through drama.

With these two short lyrics in mind we can see how a slightly longer poem, "The Need of Being Versed in Country Things," extends our sense of how Frost varies and complicates his treatment of deprived experience—the diminished thing:

> The house had gone to bring again
> To the midnight sky a sunset glow.
> Now the chimney was all of the house that stood,
> Like a pistil after the petals go.
>
> The barn opposed across the way,
> That would have joined the house in flame
> Had it been the will of the wind, was left
> To bear forsaken the place's name.
>
> No more it opened with all one end
> For teams that came by the stony road
> To drum on the floor with scurrying hoofs
> And brush the mow with the summer load.
>
> The birds that came to it through the air
> At broken windows flew out and in,
> Their murmur more like the sigh we sigh
> From too much dwelling on what has been.
>
> Yet for them the lilac renewed its leaf,
> And the aged elm, though touched with fire;
> And the dry pump flung up an awkward arm;
> And the fence post carried a strand of wire.
>
> For them there was really nothing sad.
> But though they rejoiced in the nest they kept,
> One had to be versed in country things
> Not to believe the phoebes wept.

Each of the first four stanzas describes either a frustrated or a successful meeting between country things, and through images

of desolation expresses what is entailed in such a meeting. The
speaker animates his objects by using active verbs and by allowing
them the illusion of choice: "the house had gone to bring again,"
and "the barn . . ./. . . would have joined." Paraphrased in terms
of "meetings" the argument runs something like this: the burning
house fuses with the sky in that "sunset glow" which makes it no
longer a house but a forsaken pistil; the barn unsuccessfully attempts to meet the house in its destruction and is left as a barren
reminder of the place—it can no longer meet the teams which
carry hay to it, and it meets the birds only through the defective
broken windows that are left. The birds' "murmur" is taken to be
their sad comment on the desolate scene, and by the end of stanza
four we have moved into the realm of human grief; the sound of
the birds' flight is like our sighs over things departed. Although
this simile is introduced quietly enough it is important to the
meaning of the poem. Frost is concerned with exploring the implications of meeting through simile; the murmur of birds and human
sighing come together through the pleasant ambiguity of "dwelling" as the birds literally enact what the mind is engaged in. And
the sound of "Their murmur more like the sigh we sigh" in its
alliteration, assonance and repetition contributes nicely to the
melancholy identification in grief which the speaker momentarily
asks us to accept.

That the identification is a momentary one, though, is immedi-
ately apparent by the fifth stanza as the phrase "Yet for them . . ."
introduces a distinction between the birds and ourselves which the
remainder of the poem fills out. It becomes evident that Frost is
playing a double game here. He draws on the pastoral situation
which is typically concerned with the occurrence of certain meetings in nature: the shepherd's lament is expressed through the
sympathetic participation of the objects around him. So, in this
poem, the objects actively engage in their various renewals and
the narrator continues to endow these actions with willful purpose;
they are performed for the sake of the phoebes. Yet at the same
time Frost is engaged, delicately and tenderly to be sure, in a
criticism of the pastoral mode, more specifically the process of
sympathetic identification between man and nature that Ruskin
termed the "pathetic fallacy." This fallacy is committed gram-
matically at the end of the fourth stanza by the deliberately loose
identification of human beings and phoebes: "Their murmur more
like the sigh we sigh." The word "more" here does not refer

precisely to anything but aptly conveys the temptation to see one's feelings expressed by the surrounding natural objects.

But as the speaker observes (in stanza five) various remarkable ways in which nature renews itself he is made conscious of the large difference between himself and the phoebes which his earlier simile did not express. The adaptation that a ruined nature can make is cause for surprise if not admiration, but it can adapt insofar as it does not and cannot show ". . . too much dwelling on what has been." When the speaker at the end of "Hyla Brook" salutes the things for what they are, he is refusing to dwell on the brook as it once was by accepting the present diminished thing. In this poem the catalogue of natural renewals forces the speaker to admit that "For them there was really nothing sad"; it is this knowledge that contends with the attractive temptation to read human regrets into the non-human. Indeed the poem is about more than one "need," and both of these tendencies are admirably expressed in the last stanza:

> For them there was really nothing sad.
> But though they rejoiced in the nest they kept,
> One had to be versed in country things
> Not to believe the phoebes wept.

Here we have a fine example of the way the tone of a passage can work against its prose sense, or at least communicate to a reader everything that a simple paraphrase leaves out. "Really" is not a word to which Frost as poet is addicted, and his use of it in this passage is deliberately rhetorical, conveying as it does the reluctance with which this truth about the phoebes is admitted. We ordinarily use the word in a strongly emotive sense to invoke the case which is true, no matter how strongly the immediate situation might seem to contradict it—"but really, you know, there's nothing there at all." As Frost uses it, "really" carries a rather wistful distant quality of admission which is promptly qualified by the following "But though. . . ." The truth of "rejoiced" is clear and undeniable as a statement about the phoebes' situation; at the same time the tone and grammar make a maximum case for the pathetic fallacy that is rejected. "One had" suggests both the difficulty and tentativeness of being so "versed," and the poem ends with "wept" although we know that this is contrary to fact.

The poem is a tender criticism of pastoral because it puts before us a living sense of what the much maligned pathetic fallacy can mean (in both its terms) and it does this with sureness and economy. Being versed in country things is like knowing in singing not to sing and loving things for what they are; the "wisdom" of "The Need . . ." is a sad wisdom which only just succeeds in displacing the loving untruth that opposes it. Yvor Winters' argument that Frost "believes that impulse is trustworthy and reason contemptible"[2] makes little sense in the light of this poem, which places so carefully the claims of impulse and knowledge.

III

These three poems define a central attitude toward experience which we encounter in Frost's poetry, an attitude that can be found in a poem as early as "Reluctance" and which reaches full articulation in later ones like "The Most of It" and "Directive." I am not bent on classifying or reducing the pleasure and variety we receive from the poetry under the heading of any single large attitude; but one poem does imply another, and schematism is helpful as long as we remain conscious of our schemes. The attitude is elusive, but Randall Jarrell has given it a fine statement in his essay "The Other Frost":

> . . . many of these poems are extraordinarily subtle and strange, poems which express an attitude that, at its most extreme, makes pessimism seem a hopeful evasion; they begin with a flat and terrible reproduction of the evil in the world and end by saying: It's so, and there's nothing you can do about it; and if there were, would *you* ever do it? The limits which existence approaches and falls back from have seldom been stated with such bare composure.[3]

"Flat and terrible reproduction of . . . evil" is not the right label for poems as discreet and artful as the ones we have examined, but the first and last parts of Jarrell's remarks are relevant, for it is precisely by the stating and acceptance of limits that Frost shows pessimism to be an evasion. Time and again in his poetry

---

[2] *The Function of Criticism: Problems and Exercises* (Denver, 1957), 179.
[3] *Poetry and the Age* (New York, 1955), 27-28.

an experience which might have culminated in lamentation or prayer is turned instead into an occasion for knowledge. Once the speaker is made aware of the distinction between himself and, say, the phoebes, or between his idea of what a brook should be and what one is actually like, or between the song of other birds and the particular sound of the oven bird, then he is no longer in danger of being overwhelmed by confusion.

In a late poem called "One Step Backward Taken" the speaker feels his position threatened by an encroaching landslide:

> But with one step backward taken
> I saved myself from going.
> A world torn loose went by me.
> Then the rain stopped and the blowing
> And the sun came out to dry me.

This concern is given its fullest, most moving treatment in "Directive," a poem from Frost's last published volume, *Steeple Bush* (1947). Here the backward step is an immense one, taken through nature and history into a new world—"Back out of all this now too much for us." The reader becomes an imagined traveler, directed through a series of monuments—geologic, historical, domestic— until he reaches the ultimate goal of the journey, a brook which the guide presents in this manner:

> I have kept hidden in the instep arch
> Of an old cedar at the waterside
> A broken drinking goblet like the Grail
> Under a spell so the wrong ones can't find it,
> So can't get saved, as Saint Mark says they mustn't.
> (I stole the goblet from the children's playhouse.)
> Here are your waters and your watering place.
> Drink and be whole again beyond confusion.

In these final lines of the poem what had been referred to earlier as "Your destination and your destiny" come together as the guide reveals himself to be a wizard who makes use of magic places and spells to guarantee the effectiveness of his cure. By moving back to the source and drinking the waters out of a goblet like the Grail, the traveler will be transformed, miraculously "whole again beyond confusion." Salvation from the "now too much for us" is achieved by a private act in which the "momentary stay against confusion" seems to be transformed into a permanent condition "beyond confusion" as the Christian sacramental character of the act would transcend nature and time.

But while this ritual is being performed the language undercuts it and makes it into something else than a Christian salvation. Looking at the kind of refreshment the guide holds up, we see that the goblet is a broken one, stolen from the children's playhouse; and we are forced to reconsider this salvation in the light of the strange circumstances under which it is offered. For the traveler-reader has been taken so far out of "this now too much for us," so far "beyond confusion" that in a rather frightening sense anything goes. Is there any distinction, Frost seems to be asking, between a solemn act of faith and the wildest scheme of make-believe? He imagines a state beyond the confusion of history and personality as well, yet we are permitted to experience this state only through the accents of a voice that is priest, magician, rural humorist, child and spellbinder all at the same time. In other words, salvation, as it is put forth by the guide, is inseparable from a very elaborate and peculiar tone of voice, establishing itself in every line and forcing the reader continually to adjust his sense of the way something is being said.

The difficulty presented by the end of "Directive" is mainly a matter of deciding how to "take" the goblet, the salvation which is offered to us. We can usefully distinguish Frost's expression of salvation from that of Eliot, in the conclusion to "Little Gidding":

> We shall not cease from exploration
> And the end of all our exploring
> Will be to arrive where we started
> And know the place for the first time.
> Through the unknown, remembered gate
> When the last of earth left to discover
> Is that which was the beginning;
> At the source of the longest river
> The voice of the hidden waterfall
> And the children in the apple-tree
> Not known, because not looked for
> But heard, half-heard, in the stillness
> Between two waves of the sea.
> Quick now, here, now, always—
> A condition of complete simplicity
> (Costing not less than everything) . . .

Many of the props in this first world are similar to those of "Directive," and the voice in "Little Gidding" tells us that we shall arrive where we started, back to a condition of complete simplicity which costs everything and which is absolutely worth it. An unchanging voice steadily delineates the qualities of the state of the soul ready for salvation; the voice imagines for us what redemption will be like, and is thoroughly and straightforwardly expressive of where one must be to achieve it. Hugh Kenner remarks that "The end of 'Little Gidding' fends off nothing"[4] and it is precisely this complete openness to the transforming experience that Eliot's tone conveys.

In "Directive" the guide's relationship to the waters he offers is a trickier matter. Do we end up with salvation or make-believe? Are we invited to recreate ourselves or to annihilate ourselves? These questions are ways of asking the larger question of whether we are to take "Directive" as a religious preparation for transformation or a heartbreaking joke on the very solace it puts forth. Surely it is tone that makes all the difference. Putting the voice of "Directive" next to the one we have at the end of "Little Gidding," we can see that there is nothing in or out of the world that can reduce Frost to a monotone, since he is never wholly caught up and taken in by his own offer. In one last great poetic effort he sets out to imagine an undiminished nature so perfectly appropriate to the mind that there is, seemingly, no difference between desire and fulfillment. Yet, there persists a play of voice which fends off everything by insisting that there is *all* the difference between the mind and what is outside it, and that this very difference makes the use of imagination possible and necessary. In the earlier poems considered, the "one step backward taken" is a modest but significant step back from the danger of confusion to the relative safety of knowledge—to that clarification of life which Frost defines as the end of poems. "Directive," like the earlier poems, "ends in wisdom" by suggesting that there is a time, perhaps, when the backward step is necessary to save us from salvation itself.

---

[4] *The Invisible Poet: T. S. Eliot* (New York, 1959), 323.

3. Epilogue: A Configuration of Order

Alfred Kazin

The Strength of Robert Frost

Between 1954 and 1958, first in Northampton, then at Amherst, I saw Robert Frost often in the setting of a New England college town. In his eighties his presence was strong, vivid, gifted, contradictory, and passionate; I was fascinated by his sense of himself. He was continually presenting himself to professors and to students, filling them in on his life, expounding his views, reading his poems, and could get dangerously flushed with the excitement of "saying" these poems and then taking off from them for general remarks to people who were always younger than himself, dazzled by so much temperament, force, obstinacy, and intelligence. However, his own remarks, even when they were connected only by reference to his own career, were in detail usually close in thought, pithy, original in expression, and wildly felt; he was a startling unison of intellectual passion and of a sensibility still raw in its memories of pain.

Frost was very gifted, proud, honest, ambitious, religious, and mischievous. He was a figure of perilous balances and unyielding

From *Commentary* XXXVIII (December, 1964), 49-52. Reprinted from *Commentary*, by permission; Copyright © 1964 by the American Jewish Committee.

memories who seemed held together by his fierce pride as a crafts-
man and thinker. There was nothing in the local English depart-
ments that he did not want to know about or even take a hand
in, and any professor of American literature, any critic or scholar
who would be likely to write about him, was encouraged and
informed with a matter-of-fact regard for his own fame and a
shrewd interest in promoting it that was not without pride in
what he could do for scholars. But shrewdly and paternally as
he handled his admirers, he would respond to the mention of any
other celebrated figure in contemporary literature with a guarded-
ness, destructive gossip, and sometimes open anger that his own
fiercely cherished place was being invaded in conversation. He was
always irritable and resentful about Ezra Pound, who in 1913 had
been among the first in London to praise Frost's first book,
A Boy's Will, but had done this with such a possessive air that
Frost had never been able to forgive him any more than he could
forgive Pound his impresario's temperament, his contempt for
American culture, his faking as a classical scholar, and his fame
among the avant-garde.

Frost could be very puritanical about the celebrated; all he
would say about Faulkner, after they had gone down to Latin
America together on a cultural mission for the State Department,
was that the novelist was "intemperate." If the listener took this
as an unexpressed suggestion about Faulkner's novels—Frost had
a poet's disapproval of fiction anyway as lacking true style—Frost
would not exert himself to limit the criticism. He had the almost
physical repulsion of other temperaments that often, not always,
comes with very powerful imaginative capacity. He was just the
opposite of the scholars and critics with whom he spent much of
his time, for he was by no means prepared to consider another's
opinion just because it had been published. His own critical thinking was original, speculative, fiercely practical, based on the principles he had worked out in defense of his own creative mission
as a poet seeking to approximate the spoken language; younger
poets he noticed chiefly when they evaded the test of skill, lacked
dramatic tone and "sparkle," or slipped into liberal or radical
postures that he despised as defeatism confusing itself into utopi-
anism. The wildly self-assertive strength that I always saw in him,
even when he was doing nothing but fend off questions that were
useless to him, was his prime test of a man and his opinions.
Strength he valued more than anything else, and he gave it a
kind of metaphysical status in the universe at large. "Style is the

way a man takes himself," he had written in an introduction to
Edwin Arlington Robinson's *King Jasper;* it was one of his few
published tributes to another poet.

Frost could be very scornful about positions that he disliked;
in the 50's, before John F. Kennedy came into his life and gave
him such a new sense of power and importance that Frost began
to feel that he, too, was part of the age of space and so gave his
benediction to expanding government action, he was waspish and
petty still about the most desperately needed social legislation of
the 30's. Frost's politics were certainly conservative, if not as
violently right-wing as some opinions in his family. Frost himself
had the characteristic bitterness of the old-stock American who
feels that he is being forced to pay for "alien" welfare schemes
created to take care of the lazy and the incompetent. His real
political hero was Senator Taft, who was also civilized enough to
admire his poetry. Frost was very personal about people in office;
just as Napoleon vaguely resented writers for being so ambitious,
so Frost was prepared to admire "rulers" for being as strong-
minded as writers. But until Eisenhower was finally prodded by
Sherman Adams into inviting Frost to the White House, Frost
was bitter that Eisenhower should have been indifferent to him
and that the President preferred to associate with business execu-
tives. Kennedy's admiration helped to make Frost "a Democrat
again."

Listening to Frost talk about politicians and politics in his way,
I came to admire him for his fierce self-regard more than I would
have expected to; whether cause or effect or accompanying condition, it was certainly connected with his great gift. A very old,
swollen, slowly moving man, he defended every particle of existence left to him and remembered every grief with a depth of
feeling for those he had lost; the subtlety and hardness of his
thinking were particularly striking in the company of people
always concessive, watchful, neutral, and subdued. He was from
another species, where people were smarter but also not afraid
to suffer. He was openly vulnerable. In the candid commentary
to his large volume of selected Frost letters,* Professor Lawrance
Thompson, Frost's designated biographer, contrasts Frost's lack
of confidence with his strong pride in himself as a poet. Frost
gave the impression of fighting to keep everything he had won,

* *Selected Letters of Robert Frost,* edited by Lawrance Thompson, Holt,
Rinehart & Winston.

of having to triumph over every obstacle, of wanting to call on everything within reach for his continuing education. Of course I had known about Frost's early difficulties in getting a hearing, and that it was only in England, when he was thirty-nine, that he was able to get his first book published; I knew that he relished his many academic honors all the more because of his own brief and irregular attempts at a college education. But it was startling to find Frost reciting all his early college grades and still cursing Pound for a braggart as he walked up and down the cold Amherst streets after he had had a too exciting evening reading from his poems in Johnson Chapel and could not sleep. He would recite his life over again, exactly as he does in so many letters to scholars, critics, reviewers, and collectors in Professor Thompson's book. Yet the most extraordinary thing about his verbal memories was the spell they put on him as he recited them. The transitions were as wonderful, original, and clairvoyant as they are in his best poems; even when he was shaking with fatigue and cold but would obstinately refuse to go to bed until he had talked himself out, his ideas were sinewy, shrewd, right on the button. I understood better why Frost felt related to Emerson, despite the difference in their philosophies. One of Emerson's early biographers remembers him talking in a stream of perfect sentences even when he was dying. Frost's sentences were achieved definitions, and showed an obsessive drive to clarity. One felt that they were a physical necessity.

In quarters naturally hostile to poetry that requires intellectual effort, Frost enjoyed a misleading reputation as a poet accommodating to average capacities and prejudices. Actually Frost had a bleak, if stoical, outlook; the religious faith which in private came out like the most stubborn of his loves was perhaps more a fact in Frost's complicated personal strategy for living than in his work, which in its best period did not seek to express personal beliefs, but dramatized concrete situations as new material for poetry. What makes Frost's poetry unusually interesting to the general reader is Frost's subject matter, which is characteristic experience in dramatic encounters. Frost does not write about poetry or about making the modern world safe for poetry, the usual themes of romantic and symbolist poets, for whom the poet himself is the hero. Frost writes about situations which threaten the moral balance of the passerby who has fallen into the situation. He makes poetry out of the dramatic, startling contest with the negative blackness that begins everywhere outside the hard-won human order. Frost's poetry is about the strength needed for living one's life, and it is about living in a way that differs very sharply from the stock poetry of modern life as a tragedy of disbelief, from the self-conscious ironies of literary reference that make the poet sound like Hamlet talking to Polonius.

To read Frost's best poems is to have a series of satisfactions in the intellectual, emotional, and technical conquest of difficulties. They certainly do not inspire the reader with the wonder of pure imagination that is found in Yeats; even Hardy, whom we inevitably think of when reading Frost, gives the reader a sense of the Biblical cosmos, the more-than-human significance of the creation itself, that we do not find extending out of Frost's dramatic narratives. Frost's poems are directly about struggle; the terms of the struggle are defined with satisfying honesty and exactness, even to the epistemological difficulties that man encounters in getting to know the world. One feels in reading Frost's best pieces that he has defined certain difficulties of existence exactly, and has solved them just in the nick of time, so that little is left over for man's imaginative edification. Poetry now exists as if to assure us of another world, more worthy of our imagination; and when Eliot or Stevens actually makes us see this other world, we are dazed and grateful, as if the gold diffused in the sea had solidified and were now shining in our eyes. But Frost, who said that Stevens wrote on bric-a-brac, wanted to make poetry the triumph of this world. His hand-carved poems came out without the slightest concession to elegance, and the imaginative splendor he achieved, deeply impressive but by no means meant to impress you with splendor anywhere else, lay in the idiosyncratic truth of his lines, in the depth of experience that we associate with such masterful ability to achieve transitions. Just as Frost's God did not seem to extend *to* the world, so that He held the balance of existence but would not influence it, so Frost's poems do not make living easier, or imaginatively more luxurious. But they are immensely satisfying, because of the voice that prevails in them.

The Frost I briefly knew fought for fame, for control of his reputation, for mastery of human experience, on terms which he seemed able to impose on the younger and more passive people around him. So in this book of his letters, one hears Frost talking about his own life, advancing his career, handling the many people who were useful to him. A letter for Frost was an exercise in assertion, without the charm that the interplay of poetic narrative called out of him. Frost did not like writing letters and he did not surrender to anything when he wrote one. But the letters together make an impressive account of Frost's efforts to establish himself and to uphold himself. The severity of his struggles stuck to him in his triumph and became for him the characteristic mark of triumph.

Frost was born in San Francisco because his father, who sympathized with the Confederacy and named him after Robert E. Lee, was trying to make good as a journalist and editor away from his New England family. The father died of tuberculosis in his thirties, and the mother, a native of Scotland, then followed the body of her husband back East, where she taught in the public schools and eventually opened a school of her own in order to support the children. She educated Frost at home until he was ready for high school in Lawrence, Massachusetts. Frost tried Dartmouth for less than a semester, worked as a light-trimmer and gate-tender in the Lawrence mills, and was married at twenty-one to the remarkable girl who had been his fellow-valedictorian in high school. When he was already a father, he tried Harvard for a while as a special student, then withdrew. His crucial period was the nine years he spent on a farm in Derry, New Hampshire, where he wrote many of the poems that were to go into his first three books, *A Boy's Will, North of Boston, Mountain Interval*. At a time when so many Americans from the rural areas were fitting themselves to the new urban pace, Frost, with a large family, was living in a corner of rural New England among farmers and small villagers whose speech fascinated him and whose difficulties became material for his poetry. He was to say later that the beauty of his first poems was "the unforced expression of a life I was forced to live," and he was proud that he had learned to "perform in a language absolutely unliterary." He would occasionally get a poem published in *The Independent*, but he remained unknown and virtually unpublished until he took his family to England in 1912. He found friends and admirers among the younger English poets, and encouraged Edward Thomas to write poetry. Thomas, who was to die in the war, became the closest friend that Frost was ever to have.

Frost returned from England in 1915 to find more interest in his work here than he had ever known before, and he was soon on his way to the many triumphs and honors that were to become such a fixture of his later life. But he was never to forget his long struggle for recognition, and at the height of his fame pursued it eagerly, while he blamed his many family tragedies on the new way of life that his success had imposed on them all. "All this sickness and scatteration of the family . . . a result and a judgment on us. We ought to have gone back to farming years ago or we ought to have stayed farming when we knew we were well off."

Of course Frost knew that the times had changed for everyone as well as for himself. The loneliness and mishaps of the farm folk among whom he lived in Derry, the deserted farms and lilac-choked cellars he had written about, were themselves instances of the cost of failure among those who could or would not join the bandwagon of progress. By the 30's the penalty for such failure would be multiplied in the millions. But Frost himself could not fail now and certainly would not tolerate failure. The many failures in the 30's perhaps frightened Frost even more than the new spirit of governmental intervention outraged him. Frost had an almost physical horror of anyone admitting defeat; a famous progressive educator once spoke to him of a school he had had to close as his "fourth failure," and Frost quoted this to me with indignation. Americans were not allowed to fail and America was not allowed to fail; if Roosevelt or anybody else in power spoke of America having failed in any particular, he was a weakling and in spirit a traitor.

As shown again by his letters on the subject of writers who went "left" in the 30's, Frost could be spiteful and unrealistic about the social crisis. He was also under the inflicted guilt in those years of mental illness, death, and suicide among his children; his morale was at its lowest after the death of his wife in 1938. And despite his established and almost official position as a poet, his work meant less to "crisis" readers following after Eliot than it had to the generation of the 20's delighted by his use of plain speech. At a time when his conservatism put him at odds with many other writers, he demanded more submission as a sign of his continued importance. He certainly enjoyed his power to dominate people in his circle, and infuriated Bernard De Voto by gossiping that De Voto's analyst had advised him not to see Frost, a personality too strong for him. Frost also kept collectors on the line, both for money and the maximum assurance of future fame. He became so valuable to collectors that he complained that he was getting nervous having to watch over his waste basket and his old, disowned poems in print. Yet considering some of the bargaining and maneuvering he went in for, it is remarkable how detached, as an artist, Frost remained in his last years. His poems were getting more discursive, but his hold on everything he claimed and on everybody near him was as fierce as ever. He was endlessly involved with American colleges and universities, collectors, lectures, readings, national figures.

Kennedy's admiring interest in him, climaxed by his unforgettable reading of "The Gift Outright" at the 1961 inauguration after the fierce winter sunlight kept him from reading the new poem he had composed for the occasion, must have seemed to Frost like the last true prize of his life. In a letter to Eisenhower, he had addressed him as the "ruler" of the greatest nation in the world; he would now help to rule with the new ruler, in a new era of "poetry and power." He was in Russia for eleven days on a cultural mission, but on his return waited in vain for Kennedy to see him. Apparently he irritated Kennedy by projecting onto Khrushchev the statement that the United States would never fight. The statement Frost gave the New York *Times* was that "Khrushchev said he feared for us modern liberals. He said we were too liberal to fight. I suppose he thought we'd stand there for the next hundred years saying, 'On the one hand—but on the other hand.'" Professor Thompson says in his editorial notes: "There were others who suspected that RF might have put the phrase 'too liberal to fight' into Khrushchev's mouth to unburden RF's own conservative and familiar obsession for equating 'liberal' with 'cowardly.'"

The last time I saw Frost was in the spring of 1958, when he came back from Washington believing that his intervention with the Department of Justice had alone obtained Pound's release from St. Elizabeth's Hospital. Professor Thompson's material on Frost's part in the Pound case shows that Frost was brought in by Archibald MacLeish, who perhaps felt that his own political credit with the Eisenhower administration was not enough to help Pound. He drafted an appeal to the government signed by Frost, Hemingway, and Eliot. But Frost was sure that he had got Pound out. He sat in the President's house at Amherst talking with pride of what he had done for Pound, whom he disliked as much as ever. Pound's political views seemed to Frost just the marks of an exaggerated and disordered personality. Although he hadn't seen Pound in many years, he still felt troubled and

threatened by Pound's excessiveness. By his intervention with
Eisenhower's Attorney General, he had put order to what had
been disorder, he had helped to close the case. He was proud of
what he had done for Pound precisely because he disliked him;
he had disciplined himself, and in a sense he had helped to
administer a lesson to Pound, whether Pound knew it or not.
"I did it," he said in pride and exhaustion, "I went right in
there, to the office of the Attorney General, and I talked to him."
Then he made a face. "That Ezra," he said.